Tarot Unveiled:
The Method To its Magic

Laura E. Clarson

edited by
Phyllis B. Moore

U.S. GAMES SYSTEMS, INC.
Publishers   Stamford, CT 06902 USA

Published by U.S. Games Systems, Inc.
179 Ludlow Street
Stamford, CT 06902 USA
ISBN 0-88079-356-2
under license from Visionary Enterprises, Inc.
P.O. Box 38296
Dallas, Texas 75238
ISBN 0-945766-11-4

The Hanson-Roberts Tarot deck by Mary Hanson-Roberts.

Cover design by Suzanne Dreskin.

10 9 8 7 6 5 4

Printed in the United States of America.

Library of Congress Catalog Card Number: 89-83840

The following videotapes by Laura Clarson are available from Visionary Video Productions:

Beginning Tarot
The Minor Arcana
Intermediate Tarot
Advanced Tarot
The Astrology of Romance
Basic Handwriting Analysis — Part I
Basic Numerology — Part I
How to Read Playing Cards

Table of Contents

The Major Arcana

Combinations

Reading Spreads

The Ethics of Reading for Others

The Unknowable

Introduction

What is the Tarot?

The origins of the Tarot deck are shrouded in mystery. The time, place, and circumstances of its creation are largely a matter of speculation. Some people believe the deck dates back to Egyptian and Sumerian civilizations, where the ancients used it to symbolize the secret teachings of their mystery religions. The most popular belief is that Tarot cards were brought to Europe by fortunetelling gypsies coming from either Egypt or India. In any case, the cards were widespread in Italy, France, and Germany by the late 14th century.

The Tarot deck consists of 78 cards, including 56 Minor Arcana cards and 22 Major Arcana cards.

The **Minor Arcana** is very much like an ordinary deck of playing cards. There are four suits, each numbered from Ace to King. The Jack in traditional playing cards is called a Page in the Tarot deck. In addition, the Tarot deck includes four Knights which were dropped from the present day deck of playing cards.

The four suits in the Tarot deck are Swords, Cups, Rods, and Pentacles. In a deck of playing cards, Swords correspond to Spades, Cups to Hearts, Rods to Clubs, and Pentacles to Diamonds. **Swords** involve intellectual matters and discord, struggle, and strife. **Cups** deal with emotions and affairs of the heart. **Rods** (also called Wands) relate to enterprise, creativity, and energy. **Pentacles** (sometimes referred to as Discs) relate to money and business affairs.

The **Major Arcana** begins with the Fool and ends with the World. Of the 22 Major Arcana cards, only the Fool in the form of the Joker has survived in present-day playing cards. These cards symbolize the growth and evolution of consciousness and spiritual awareness. Their meanings are deep and refer more to psychological and spiritual levels than to everyday events of life.

When reading Tarot cards, the meanings of **upright** cards (right side up) and **reversed** cards (upside down) are different.

The reversed meaning is not always the opposite of the upright meaning. Sometimes the reversed meaning is ''too much of a good thing.'' For example, the Empress means abundance when it is upright but laziness and extravagance when reversed.

Usually, when the upright meaning involves a difficult situation or problem, the reversed meaning is better because it shows the difficulty has been overcome. For example, the Five of Pentacles means unemployment and financial insecurity when upright. Reversed it means returning to work or to financial security.

Reversed cards are represented in this book by the letter R following the card name. For example, Empress R and Five of Pentacles R stand for the reversed positions of those respective cards.

How the Tarot Works

Learning Tarot is like learning a foreign language. The individual cards are the words provided by the personal and collective unconscious. A Tarot reader translates these unconscious words into a form our conscious minds can understand. The combined access to the personal and collective unconscious is the secret to the Tarot's "magical" accuracy.

The **personal unconscious** contains everything we have experienced, even subliminally, from birth on. It stores every sensation, dream, emotion, and perception of our personal history. Through hypnosis, therapists have been able to tap into the personal unconscious to help people understand themselves better. The Tarot is a more accessible and effective tool to unlock the secrets of the personal unconscious.

The **collective unconscious** is the common pool of human experience from man's distant origins to the present. We share this inherited knowledge with all humanity, much as the animal kingdom possesses instincts. Jung discovered in working with his patients' dreams that certain mythological motifs surfaced spontaneously without any previous knowledge of the myth involved. For example, people with no exposure whatsoever to mythological lore would dream of Pan, the ancient god of nature. Jung theorized that all human beings have access to a shared heritage of human thought and experience. He called this heritage the collective unconscious.

The Tarot works by accessing what we already know unconsciously about ourselves and our destiny. When we focus on our question and shuffle the cards, we unconsciously put the cards in the precise order that will give us the answer we seek. The mysterious part of ourselves that holds all the unconscious answers may be considered our Soul or True Self. A Tarot reader is simply someone trained to understand and interpret the ancient language of the Soul.

The Language of Tarot

Because we are learning a new language when we study the Tarot, how we define the words, grammar, and syntax is important. A language is only as precise as the meanings given each word. In the language of the Tarot, our words are the upright and reversed meanings we give each card. We must give clear, non-ambiguous meanings to each card. Then, when a card appears in a spread, we can understand the message it is trying to communicate. We don't want to employ a "dead" language like Latin, with words for "forced marches" but no word for "computers." For this reason, this book contains new, updated meanings of cards for 20th-century usage. For example, meanings have been assigned for modern day phenomena such as high technology, meditation, and psychotherapy. These meanings give the unconscious the tools to speak to us in our modern, everyday language.

Starting Out

Choosing and Storing a Deck

Choose a Tarot deck that is fairly traditional in the symbols or pictures appearing on the cards. There are many newer decks that have greatly altered the original symbols. Avoid using one of those decks because it can confuse a beginning student. Be sure to select a deck in which the Minor Arcana cards show pictures of people or scenes instead of just showing the number of Cups, Swords, Rods or Pentacles. Pictures help you remember and associate meanings with the cards.

This book is illustrated with the **Hanson-Roberts** deck. The cards in this deck have a certain magical and enchanted quality that many people find appealing. Its images are also faithful to traditional Tarot symbolism. Other decks commonly used to begin learning Tarot are:

- The **Aquarian** deck
- The **Rider Waite** deck
- The **Morgan Greer** deck

When not using your deck, store the cards in a silk scarf or a box to protect them from external vibrations. Don't be concerned about other people shuffling your deck. This is fine. In fact, it is best if the person asking the question shuffles the cards. If you are concerned about this issue, however, you may want to keep a deck just for your personal use.

Breaking in a New Deck

To break in a new deck of cards, sleep with it under your pillow or next to your bed for the first few weeks. This blends your energies with the cards. You might try cutting the cards every morning when you wake up. Look up the meaning of the card you select, and use it as an indicator of events or an attitude for the day. This is a good way to start learning the meanings of the cards and applying them to your life.

How to Shuffle

Since you will be reading both upright and reversed cards in spreads, shuffle the cards in such a way that some will be upright and some reversed. Shuffle like this as many times as feels right for you. Some readers use a set number of shuffles and cuts. Others shuffle until the cards feel hard to push back together, then stop without cutting. What is important is that you consistently use the same system every time you shuffle.

How to Deal

When the cards are ready to be dealt, be sure you deal them from the side. Don't turn them over from bottom to top because this will reverse the meanings of the cards.

Phrasing the Question

Let's suppose you want to ask the Tarot about changing jobs. Don't ask too narrow a question such as ''Will I make more money at XYZ company?'' Also avoid asking a yes or no question such as ''Should I change jobs?'' It is better to phrase the question more generally. For example, ''Please give me information about my going to work at XYZ company.'' This allows the cards to describe the past, present, and future of the situation without being confined to one facet of the question or just a yes or no answer.

Your Attitude Before Consulting the Cards

To focus your mind and clear any distractions before reading the cards, silently say to yourself any prayer, invocation, or mantram of your choosing before beginning. Ask for guidance and insight to interpret the cards accurately and wisely.

The Tarot should be approached seriously with humility, just as you would approach a wise teacher or counselor for advice about a problem in your life. Never test the Tarot by asking the same question over and over again. The first answer is usually the most revealing. You can ask about different facets of the same question or wait a week or so to repeat the question. In that interval, things related to the situation may have changed somewhat so that repeating the question is appropriate.

When you first begin reading Tarot cards, it is best to write down the questions and the cards you receive as answers.

How to Draw Your Own Associations About the Cards

The best way to learn Tarot is to draw your own personal associations about the cards. Use the symbols on the cards to trigger insights and open your intuitive powers. Personalize each card as much as possible by associating with it your personal experiences along with the meanings given in this book.

For example, the Tower card in the Major Arcana deals with situations when plans fall apart, abrupt changes take place, and unexpected shocks occur. The Tower represents the crumbling of your sense of security. When you see this card, go back over your life and recall a time when you felt as if "the rug were pulled out from under you" suddenly and unexpectedly. This will call up feelings, memories, and emotions you can relate to the card instead of just trying to remember a pat meaning from a book.

Building a Tarot Notebook

It's a good idea to buy a special notebook for your Tarot studies. Devote a page to each card. Taking one at a time, read the meaning, look at the picture and symbols and think of everything you associate with that card. Include people, events, and characters from books, movies, or TV. Give your imagination full rein. As you go through the day, something may remind you of one of the cards. Jot it down on that page. Cut out pictures from magazines that remind you of certain cards. The idea is to implant feelings about each card in your unconscious mind. Then, when you see a particular card, you get a feeling about what it means, not just a dry textbook idea.

Some cards will leave you cold and inspire nothing in you. Others you will identify with immediately. Pick the ones you identify with to relate to first. Some of the pictures depict individual people. These are the Court cards, similar to face cards in an ordinary deck. If a Court card reminds you of someone you know, let it represent that person to you.

Choosing Cards to Represent Yourself

Choose one of the Court cards to represent yourself in your everyday life. You can choose from among four Kings, Queens, Knights and Pages. Let your intuition and personal identification determine the card you pick.

Also choose a card from the Major Arcana to represent your psychological, mental, and spiritual growth. It can be any card in the Major Arcana, not necessarily one with a person pictured on it.

Testing the Validity of Your Spreads

Be cautious when you first start out reading Tarot cards not to take the answers you get as gospel. It takes time to establish a flow or rapport with the cards so that its communication is consistent. Remember not to repeat the same question right away. Write down your questions and spreads so that you can go back over them and see how accurate they were in the future. It is also a good idea to test the validity of your spread by looking at cards 1 through 5 of the Celtic Cross Spread first. See if the past and present as represented by these cards match with what you already know about the situation before you read cards 6 through 10 for future influences. If the past and present seem accurate, you can trust the accuracy of the future in the spread.

Reading for Yourself and Others

It is often more difficult to read for yourself than for another person. It requires more objectivity and the element of wishful thinking often creeps in. Reading for other people whose situations you know nothing about helps you validate the accuracy of the Tarot as a tool. However, if you're just learning Tarot, be sure to warn people of this fact.

The Minor Arcana

Overview

The Minor Arcana of the Tarot includes four suits. The general meaning of each suit and short descriptions of all the cards in each suit are presented here for quick reference. The next two chapters give more detailed meanings of the individual cards of the Minor Arcana. Those chapters are organized numerically from Ace through Ten, and Page through King, rather than by suit.

Swords

Swords

Swords involve stress, conflict, and turmoil. They indicate courage and mental energy. Upright and reversed meanings of the individual Sword cards are given here.

ACE	courageous beginning against odds; initiating necessary conflict; turmoil; intense feelings
Reversed	too forceful; pushing too hard to start something; unnecessary stirring up of conflict
2	locking horns; stalemate; truce; competitive, challenging, abrasive relationship
Reversed	resolution of conflict between forces; reconciliation; joining forces with the competition; deadlock removed
3	triangle relationship causing pain, separation, divorce, heartbreak; intense attachment
Reversed	pain going away; recovery from triangle or emotionally painful relationship
4	need for recuperation from stress; sickness; inactivity; rest from conflict; calm, quiet healing; rest and recuperation
Reversed	healing is over; ready for activity; restoration of health; recuperation complete
5	gloating enemy; unfaithful lover; jealous vindictive enemy; vicious gossip; betrayal; lack of forgiveness
Reversed	vindication and triumph over enemy and over gossip and betrayal; forgiveness
6	helpful assistance in strife; turmoil subsiding; problems can be worked out; bridge over troubled waters; travel over water
Reversed	heading for trouble again; no immediate solution; help not accepted

Swords

7	theft; bitterness over rip off; feeling like a loser in contest; victimized; mistrust
Reversed	return of stolen property or person; unexpected triumph after a loss
8	restriction and limitation; no understanding of blocks to freedom; refusal to break chains
Reversed	breaking out of prison; unblocking fear of independence; seeing path to escape; overcoming outside restriction
9	worry and anxiety over worsening problems; heavy grief or depression; fear
Reversed	release of tension and worry; sunshine after storm; Thank the Lord card
10	utterly crushed and defeated by situation; divorce; bankruptcy; forced to start over
Reversed	having survived the worst that can happen; recovery from disaster; getting back on feet again
PAGE	upsetting message; sharp words; forceful communication; person under 25 who is intelligent and outspoken
Reversed	misunderstanding; angry words; argument; belligerent young person
KNIGHT	taking assertive, courageous action; outspoken strong-willed man (25-40)
Reversed	acting too pushy; conflict with an aggressive troublemaker (25-40)
QUEEN	woman who is no-nonsense, stern, strong-willed, dominating, take charge
Reversed	vindictive, jealous, petty, unforgiving, demanding woman
KING	lawyer; doctor; good mind; verbal skills; quick wit; perceptive but don't cross him; man over 40
Reversed	verbal manipulator; uses people; harsh and merciless; ruthless for power

Cups

Cups

Cups deal with emotional issues, love, family, friends and all affairs of the heart. They indicate harmony or disharmony in emotional areas. Upright and reversed meanings of the individual Cup cards are given here.

ACE	new beginning of love and emotional rapport; good karma emotionally; new love relationship or friendship
Reversed	wishing for new relationship and seeing possibility where none exists; false start; delay of new relationship
2	friendship; pleasant rapport; compatibility of emotional temperament; date
Reversed	loss of friendship; minor disputes; discord in friendship; one of parties breaking off
3	group of friends; family functions; parties; drinking; fun; entertainment; planned pregnancy
Reversed	excessive drinking, partying, overindulgence, dissipation, alcoholism; accidental pregnancy; promiscuity
4	boredom; missed opportunity; dissatisfaction; apathetic; uninspired
Reversed	accepting an opportunity; seeing the value of present situation; motivated; ready for new relationship
5	sense of loss; crying over spilled milk; feeling incomplete without someone
Reversed	appreciation of what is left over after a loss; self-reliant and self-sufficient
6	past friends; children; karmic ties (good); return of past lover or friend; gift
Reversed	need to release friends whom you have outgrown; don't let past lover return
7	confusion; fantasy; too many choices; romantic illusions; rose-colored glasses

Cups

Reversed	willing to focus on one thing or person and get realistic; focused creativity and imagination
8	withdrawing self or affections from a relationship; losing interest; backing off; loneliness; leaving stagnated situation to pursue meaningful interests
Reversed	dance-away lover; commitment phobia; fear of intimacy; settling for mediocrity; returning to situation you withdrew from
9	wish card; perfect dream come true; great enjoyment and fulfillment
Reversed	still hoping and waiting for wish to come true but wish delayed or denied; be sure to know what you want before you wish for it
10	mutual love; perfect love and happiness; rapport on all levels; totally in love; sharing
Reversed	one-sided love; areas of incompatibility; disharmony in relationship; arguments between lovers
PAGE	child; gay person; love letter or phone call; invitation for a date or party
Reversed	lack of communication from lover or friend; slow period in dating
KNIGHT	charming ladies' man who is pleasant, sensitive and emotionally warm; social invitation
Reversed	Don Juan; Romeo; charming but insincere man; uses women; love them and leave them
QUEEN	caring and nurturing woman; mother; good listener; gentle, romantic, sensitive, emotional; good counselor
Reversed	naive and vulnerable; gullible; easily influenced; friendly but superficial; sucker for a sob story
KING	nurturing father; family man; generous and protective; enjoys people work; likes helping people
Reversed	spoils people; overprotective; smothering; won't let go

Rods

Rods

Rods (or Wands) are a creative suit, and deal with inspiration, motivation, visionary causes, intuition, and enthusiasm. Upright and reversed meanings of the individual Rod cards are given here.

ACE	new ideas and creativity, beginning of enterprise or invention; creative offer
Reversed	canceling of new enterprise; false start; idea ahead of its time; delayed start
2	collaboration of ideas; creative partnership; friendship based on common cause or interest; able to communicate ideas well with other party; negotiation
Reversed	creative differences; incompatible values and goals
3	fulfillment of creative ideas; invention; making new idea work; creative flow
Reversed	still some bugs in new enterprise; delays an setbacks; creative block
4	marriage; partnership; establishment of creativ goals in workable form
Reversed	living together; dissolving partnership; change i creative goals
5	competition; disputes; lawsuit; clash of will: promotion of business
Reversed	peace after disputes; settlement of lawsuits; cooperation
6	realization of creative dreams at work, arts or sciences; pleasure and victory after hard work
Reversed	disillusionment and defeat of dreams; rewards delayed; opponent wins
7	success against opposition; position of advantage in business; victory through courage ·
Reversed	feeling threatened; losing ground; show of strength but feels inadequate

Rods

8	air travel; good news comes fast; love letters; haste; great hope; approach to a goal
Reversed	delay of travel, news or reaching goal; arrows of jealousy; stagnation of affairs
9	ready for what comes; waiting and watching; be patient; strength in reserve
Reversed	unprepared for problems that may arise; impatient; scattered energies; defensive
10	carrying heavy burden; workaholic; too much pressure and responsibility; abuse of power; all work and no play
Reversed	heavy load lifted; delegates responsibility; able to play and enjoy life now
PAGE	young person under 25 who is enthusiastic, enterprising, and creative; good news
Reversed	young person who is flighty, scatterbrained, and over-reactive; bad news
KNIGHT	man (25-40) who is energetic, hasty, ardent; spur-of-the-moment person; change of residence; travel; quick departure
Reversed	jealous lover; man who is too pushy, unreliable, inconsistent, impatient
QUEEN	woman who is creative, ardent, enthusiastic, dynamic, enterprising; bubbly personality
Reversed	woman who is flighty, scatterbrained, hysterical under pressure, always late
KING	creative man of vision who isn't afraid to risk and speculate; self-starter; open to new ideas; self-made; entrepreneur
Reversed	man who is impulsive in business decisions; falls for get-rich-quick schemes; con artist/promoter

Pentacles

Pentacles

Pentacles (or Discs) deal with practicality, money, material possessions, and are a work-oriented suit. Upright and reversed meanings of the individual Pentacle cards are given here.

ACE	new financial venture which will be beneficial
Reversed	timing wrong for initiating new venture; false start; delayed start
2	business partnership; equal division; juggling two work situations; working two jobs
Reversed	alone in business; working one job after juggling two things; settling on one venture; business decisions
3	work which is very fulfilling or best vocation; achievement of expertise
Reversed	over-qualified or bored because nothing new to learn; mediocrity; too critical of self or others
4	financially stable and secure; solid investments; concerned with money and possessions
Reversed	greedy; penny-pinching; grasping and materialistic; stingy; fear of poverty; self-protective
5	unemployed; lay off or getting fired; money very tight; freelance work; uncertain about career
Reversed	going back to work after unemployment; money coming in again; steady work; decision about career
6	good karma regarding money; universe provides; gift; loan; grant of money; benefactor
Reversed	having to repay debts; non-renewal of loan or grant; benefactor stops; support withdrawn
7	unexpected money comes in; job promotion or raise; business travel; good business investment
Reversed	unexpected shake-up in work or in finances; unexpected expense; bad business investment

Pentacles

8	learning a new skill; going to school; training; selling something
Reversed	losing interest in skill; dropping out of school; delay or slow down in sales
9	financially taken care of; buying something; solitary affluence; love of home and gardens; spending money on home, real estate, or office
Reversed	danger of burglary; house expense; financial loss; selling a house; moving an office
10	riches; inheritance; corporate prosperity; family money; a windfall or large sum of money gained
Reversed	corporate losses; heavy money losses; trouble over inheritance; family problems; forced to sell a house or land
PAGE	a scholar; good management of money by person under 25; good message about money; contracts; negotiations about money
Reversed	waste of material things; news of loss of money; young person who is self-critical
KNIGHT	hard-working, patient, responsible man (25-40); coming or going of money matters
Reversed	man who is dull, unprogressive, workaholic, and overcritical about details
QUEEN	woman who is practical, resourceful in business, well-organized, go-getter
Reversed	superficial, materialistic woman; status seeker; name dropper; wants to look rich; gold-digger
KING	business man of means; merchant or boss; banker; real estate; reliable; math and financial ability
Reversed	poor business sense; wasteful and disorganized; wheeler-dealer

Aces Through Tens

Overview

An easy way to learn the Minor Arcana cards is to understand the meanings of the numbers and blend them with the meanings of the suits.

For example, all **Aces** deal with new beginnings and initiating new projects. With that information, we can conclude that the:

- Ace of Swords has to do with new courage and taking a strong stand against odds
- Ace of Cups involves new relationships
- Ace of Rods brings in new ideas or creativity, and the
- Ace of Pentacles pertains to new financial ventures.

The same thing applies for the other numbers. All of the **Twos** deal with balancing two people, situations, or viewpoints because Two is the number of relationship and duality.

The **Threes** represent a harmony or blending of three elements, and relate to synthesis, collaboration, and self-expression. The exception is the Swords suit, where these elements are lacking, causing discord.

The **Fours** deal with foundations that have been set up and indicate stability and the status quo.

The **Fives** are volatile cards implying the necessity to adapt to unpleasant changes.

The **Sixes** indicate assistance and a change for the better. They can indicate perfection and the accomplishment of ideals.

The **Sevens** deal with new awareness and perspective. They indicate changes brought about by more insight into a situation.

The **Eights** show control, power, and mastery over a situation through self-reliance and autonomy.

The **Nines** bring completion and fulfillment of each suit. They show the maximum intensity of each suit in the cycle.

The **Tens** show renewal through a new cycle. They indicate that many lessons have been learned regarding the suit in question. They signify mastery of those lessons.

To summarize:

1 — new beginnings

2 — relationship, duality

3 — synthesis, expression

4 — foundation, stability

5 — change, instability

6 — assistance, idealism, perfection

7 — unexpected change, perception, insight

8 — control, power, organization

9 — completion, fulfillment

10 — renewal, mastery

Aces

The Ace of any suit represents raw energy in its undifferentiated form. With the Sword suit, the Ace energy is one of force and courage. With Cups, the energy is channeled into new friendships. The Ace of Rods represents the force of creativity, while the Ace of Pentacles is energy directed into a new financial enterprise.

THE ACE OF SWORDS (Courage)

UPRIGHT MEANING: This card shows a sword, similar to the sword Excalibur in the Arthurian legend, crowned with a wreath. This magical use of force and courage to achieve a lofty goal is the best application of this card's energy. The Ace of Swords is a card of intense will and determination against all odds. It may mean initiating necessary conflict in order to resolve a problem. The conflict frequently involves the use of will power and intellect, rather than physical force. The other cards in the spread will indicate the nature of the situation requiring a courageous beginning.

SUGGESTED ADVICE: This is a very positive, auspicious card for initiating new projects. It shows that the timing is right and the determination is strong to continue. Ask the client what new enterprise he is strongly motivated to begin and encourage him not to delay in acting. He must not shrink from possible turmoil and conflict arising from this new beginning. The strength of his purpose will overcome these obstacles.

REVERSED MEANING: The timing is not right for new beginnings. The client may be pushing too hard to force an issue. Too forceful a use of will at this time can operate against his desire to get started. A heavy-handed approach may stir up unnecessary conflict and backfire on the client.

THE ACE OF CUPS (New Friendships)

UPRIGHT MEANING: The water lilies beneath the chalice on this card signify the opening of the heart to new social and personal relationships. It indicates a beneficial relationship on the horizon. When this card appears in a spread with the **Two of Cups**, **Three of Cups**, **Ten of Cups** or the **Lovers** card, the beginnings of compatible and harmonious friendships are likely. Often, positive karma with a new person allows the client to feel immediately comfortable in their interaction, especially if the **Six of Cups** appears nearby. A renewal of an existing relationship is indicated if the **Eight of Cups R** or the **Three of Swords R** are also in the spread.

SUGGESTED ADVICE: Encourage the client to consider a new relationship in his life, even though he may be wary of personal attachments because of the past. Emphasize that every relationship is different, both karmically and psychologically.

REVERSED MEANING: The Ace of Cups R indicates wishful thinking on the part of the client toward a potential relationship. He may be rushing into a love affair prematurely, without taking the time to judge the appropriateness of the new person and his own needs. With favorable cards for friendship or romance in the spread, this card can simply mean that the relationship is delayed in getting off the ground.

As des Bâtons   Asso di Bastoni
Ace of Rods
Stäbe-As   As de Bastos

THE ACE OF RODS (Creativity)

UPRIGHT MEANING: The Ace of Rods shows a single rod sprouting with new life from its stalk. This card signifies new ideas and the beginning stages of creativity. Often it signals the beginning of an enterprise or a creative offer. Fiery enthusiasm, a kind of bubbling excitement, is the hallmark of an Ace of Rods type of idea or enterprise. Despite a great deal of enthusiasm and exuberance about the potential of the new enterprise, the idea could remain "just another good idea" without cards indicating practical applications, such as the **Four of Pentacles** or the **Emperor**. With the **Magician**, this card often refers to an invention or a new idea for research and development.

SUGGESTED ADVICE: The client may feel very stale and lackluster about his creativity. This card in the spread indicates that he is ready to receive inspiration from the Muse again, whether in the area of his profession, his hobbies, or other creative self-expression. This card is an encouragement to go ahead on an idea that sparks his interest.

REVERSED MEANING: The client may have an idea that is ahead of its time or one that hasn't been properly thought out. Sometimes the Ace of Rods R indicates delays in getting a new idea off the ground. This card can also refer to an idea dying on the vine before anyone ever gets around to implementing it. With the **Six of Rods R**, the **Tower**, or the **Sun R**, the Ace of Rods R can mean the canceling of a new enterprise.

THE ACE OF PENTACLES (New Financial Venture)

UPRIGHT MEANING: The flowers surrounding the pentacle on the card symbolize fruitfulness and productivity. Because this card is a Pentacle, this productivity applies to money matters. The Ace of Pentacles represents ideas relating to a new financial enterprise, which may prove very beneficial to the client. Because this card is an Ace, it carries the idea of the essential value of money and can signal an auspicious time to launch new ventures and business ideas. The surrounding cards will indicate the degree of success that can be expected from the new enterprise. The **Ten of Pentacles** or the **Empress** would herald a major triumph in business, while the returns would be more modest with the **Four of Pentacles** or the **Seven of Pentacles**.

SUGGESTED ADVICE: With positive surrounding cards in a Tarot reading, the Ace of Pentacles signifies correct timing for initiating financial changes. This is similar to the presence of positive business transits in a client's astrological chart. The client may have a business idea or opportunity he is not acting on for fear of taking a risk. Encourage him to act speedily to initiate a new business project, since the timing is right for a successful beginning.

REVERSED MEANING: The reversed position indicates delays or a false start in launching a new venture. The client would be wise to exercise patience. He must prepare himself to wait to begin the project or realize significant financial gain from it. The client may overextend himself by trying to start a business venture at an inauspicious time.

Twos

The Two of any suit represents relationships and duality. With the Sword suit, the relationship is a stalemate. With Cups, the relationship is one of friendship. The Two of Rods represents collaboration, while the Two of Pentacles stands for the balancing of two financial ventures.

THE TWO OF SWORDS
(Stalemate)

UPRIGHT MEANING: The "Catch 22" nature of this card is shown by the blindfolded woman holding two swords upright. This often refers to a person caught in the middle of a stalemate or paradoxical situation, unable to get it off hold. Usually no easy solution exists to the problem because all the possibilities are compromises. In the movement of events, this card represents ambivalence and standstill. In personal relationships, there may be an uneasy truce between two people who grate on each other's nerves. This card also connotes competitiveness and a need to "dig in your heels" until you can choose a satisfactory course of action.

SUGGESTED ADVICE: Find out who the client is locking horns with or what decision is caught on hold in his life. Caution him that he may be stubbornly refusing to see the problem or relationship in any terms but black or white. Perhaps, the deadlock can be broken by consulting an unbiased third party. Sometimes, the stalemate is circumstantial and your advice must be to weather the delay and wait for outside action.

REVERSED MEANING: This position denotes reconciliation and resolution of conflict. A decision has been made and the deadlock removed. If a difficult relationship is involved, the client has learned to adapt to the other person. The two parties can now work with instead of against each other.

Deux des Coupes • Due di Coppe
Two of Cups
Zwei-Kelche • Dos de Copas

THE TWO OF CUPS (Friendship)

UPRIGHT MEANING: This card portrays a man and woman holding cups and toasting each other. The picture shows the warmth and sharing characteristic of good rapport between people. This card relates to a one-on-one relationship between friends or lovers rather than groups of people. It shows compatibility of emotional temperaments and often relates to dating. The mutual openness and trust conveyed has the potential to develop into love. When this card appears in a spread with the **Lovers** or the **Ten of Cups**, it shows a very intense experience of true love.

SUGGESTED ADVICE: When this card appears in a spread, even in questions relating to business, a friend or lover of the client's will influence the situation. Encourage the client to value and appreciate his friends and loved ones. A compatible friend such as this one could give the client good advice on the situation. You might suggest he spend more time with his friends or on dating to balance out his life.

REVERSED MEANING: This could indicate a minor dispute or tiff between friends. Areas of incompatibility unnoticed before may be surfacing now. In a dating situation, it can mean one party is less involved or interested than the other and may break off the relationship. It shows a disparity between the way two parties in a relationship judge its value and areas of compatibility. One person may be looking at all of the areas of similarity and the other at all the areas of difference between them.

THE TWO OF RODS
(Collaboration)

UPRIGHT MEANING: The man pictured on this card holds a rod in one hand and a globe in the other. He stares into the distance with a visionary look in his eyes. The possibilities implied in this card include a collaboration of ideas and a creative partnership. This card often indicates two people of like mind joining forces for mutual benefit. It shows successful negotiation and the ability to communicate ideas well with the other party. With cards from the Cup suit, this card can relate to a friendship based on common interests or a common cause. The friends would find it very easy to share ideas in a flowing way.

SUGGESTED ADVICE: When this card appears in a spread, the client would benefit more from sharing ideas with another person than working on his own. The input and perspective to be gained from this interaction will vastly improve his chances for success. In both personal and business matters, this card indicates rewards and increased vision from comparing notes with another person.

REVERSED MEANING: This is a card of creative differences or incompatible values and goals. With the **Three of Rods R**, the **Two of Swords**, the **Five of Swords**, or the **Ten of Cups R**, there may be serious problems or violent differences involved in coming to terms with another person.

THE TWO OF PENTACLES
(Balancing Financial Affairs)

UPRIGHT MEANING: The young man pictured on this card seems very intent on keeping the two pentacles suspended in the air as a juggler would. This represents the balancing of two jobs or sources of income. By being versatile and promoting two or more business ventures, the client could benefit if he attends to the requirements of each in turn. This card often applies to a person who prefers to work two jobs because of the need for variety. If this card appears with the **Five of Pentacles**, the need for duality is more a financial necessity than a way to avoid boredom. If other favorable Pentacles appear in the spread, this card can be beneficial for business partnership. The Court cards in the spread may suggest who the possible partner is.

SUGGESTED ADVICE: Stress the financial advantages to the client of having several money-making options in his life. If he is bored with his job, perhaps a part-time second income would help relieve the tedium. Emphasize the need to be able to shift his attention easily from one project to another in order to keep up with both.

REVERSED MEANING: The Two of Pentacles R represents narrowing down several projects to one. After weighing many business alternatives, the client may decide to work on his own instead of in partnership. This card can signify that a business decision has been reached with commitment to act on it.

Threes

The Three of any suit represents synthesis and expression. With the Sword suit, this harmony is lacking, resulting in heartbreak. With Cups, the harmony is cause for celebration. The Three of Rods represents creative flow and self-expression, while the Three of Pentacles stands for mastery.

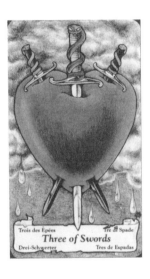

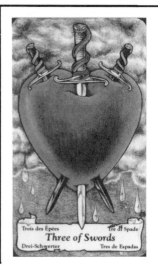

Trois des Epées   Tre di Spade
Three of Swords
Drei-Schwerter   Tres de Espadas

THE THREE OF SWORDS
(Heartbreak)

UPRIGHT MEANING: The picture conveys very clearly the intense pain associated with this card. Three swords pierce a heart, suggesting intense feelings and attachments causing deep suffering. Usually, this card relates to a crisis stemming from a relationship, such as a triangle situation, separation, or divorce. The level of pain and conflict is severe and usually the result of long-standing problems between the couple. With the **Tower, Death, Judgment**, the **Four of Rods R**, or the **Ten of Pentacles R**, a divorce is likely unless the couple seeks help to repair their differences immediately. This card can also relate to heart trouble, if combined with the **Eight of Swords**, the **Tower**, or the **Star R**.

SUGGESTED ADVICE: Often, when this card appears in a client's spread, there is a very destructive relationship involved. Intense and possessive attachment may be acting to the detriment of both parties. The client may recite a litany of abuses and transgressions which he is enduring from his partner. Ask the client what benefits he is deriving from the relationship to warrant staying in it. Often, there is a self-destructive need for both people to unconsciously enjoy some of the unhealthy aspects of the relationship. A third party is likely to be complicating the relationship; this issue needs to be discussed with the client also. Jealousy, possessiveness, and a refusal to abandon a destructive relationship figure strongly in this card's meaning.

REVERSED MEANING: This card indicates recovery from an emotionally painful relationship or a triangle and healing from emotional pain. Sometimes, it indicates the client is involved in a very difficult relationship he needs to leave, yet he doesn't realize the separation and ending will not be as painful as he thinks. He may recover very quickly once he takes the step of leaving the relationship.

THE THREE OF CUPS
(Celebration)

UPRIGHT MEANING: The three women toasting each other on this card signify a very compatible group of people, who are like family to one another if not actual family members. It is a card of fun, entertainment, parties, drinking, and conviviality, and can indicate a family reunion. Happy hours, bars, and all places where people go to have a good time are related to this card. It can also mean a wedding, baptism, birth, or other happy family celebration.

This card can indicate a planned or welcomed pregnancy, especially if the **Empress** or the **Page of Cups** appears in the spread.

SUGGESTED ADVICE: Suggest to the client that he accept social invitations in the near future because parties, weddings, and so forth will be enjoyable and congenial. A family gathering at this time would bring the family closer together. If the client would like to have a child, this would be an auspicious time for conception.

REVERSED MEANING: With this card, partying and frivolity have degenerated into excessive drinking, overindulgence, and dissipation. The client is engaging in wild abandon in an attempt to escape from something. There is a danger of alcoholism if the **Moon** or the **Seven of Cups** also appear in the spread. Carelessness and sexual promiscuity could produce an unexpected pregnancy or venereal disease if the **Empress R**, **Tower**, **Moon**, or **Seven of Cups** also appear in the spread.

Trois des Bâtons   Tre di Bastoni
Three of Rods
Drei-Stäbe   Tres de Bastos

THE THREE OF RODS (Creative Flow)

UPRIGHT MEANING: The three rods pictured on this card show a creative blending of energy by combining three ideas or approaches into a workable synthesis. It is similar to a resolution reached at a committee meeting after all of the options have been explored. This card can represent fulfillment of creative ideas by arriving at the best way to make a new idea work. It can also pertain to a creative and productive joining of three persons' forces to pool their ideas and talents. The input of three people can give a greater measure of objectivity and vision to any project when this card appears upright in a spread. When this card appears in a spread with the **Magician**, it can indicate an invention with workable potential. With the **Lovers** or **Ten of Cups**, it may apply to a triangle love relationship in which all of the parties are content to share the lover with someone else.

SUGGESTED ADVICE: The group energy symbolized by this card can apply to many situations. It can indicate preferring the company of groups to one-on-one relationships. The exchange of ideas with at least two other compatible persons can lead the client to greater awareness and creative fulfillment.

REVERSED MEANING: The urge to make new ideas gel is blocked temporarily with the reversed card. There are still some flaws in the new enterprise or the client is suffering from a creative block. The surrounding cards may indicate the solution to the problem. There will likely be delays and setbacks before the client will feel he has resolved the unworkable aspects of his plans or group activities.

THE THREE OF PENTACLES
(Mastery)

Three of Pentacles

UPRIGHT MEANING: The traditional symbol for this card is a master craftsman working on a cathedral, much as Michelangelo did. The training and practice of the **Eight of Pentacles** has resulted in achievement of expertise and in mastery of a skill. This card often represents an expert in a field and great satisfaction from work. It is the card of finding one's best vocation and the most fulfilling use of one's talents. It shows a perfectionism and attention to detail that evidences a love of one's work. With the **Seven of Cups**, it can indicate creative or artistic talent. When it appears with Cups or other relationship cards, it can mean very high standards in choosing a lover. If combined with the **Hermit**, the client might consider teaching in the area of his excellence.

SUGGESTED ADVICE: Congratulate the client on his mastery and expertise in his field. He may not give himself credit for the quality of his work. There may be a possibility of marketing this area of expertise for extra income.

REVERSED MEANING: This card can relate to a person who is overqualified for his job or bored at work because there is nothing new to learn. It can also refer to a person who has settled for mediocrity and stopped short of mastery of a skill. It can also indicate a person who is too critical of himself and others. When combined with Cups, the client may be too harsh a judge of potential lovers or friends.

Fours

The Four of any suit represents foundation, stability, and the status quo. With the Sword suit, the status quo is being preserved during a period of recuperation. With Cups, the status quo is the result of apathy. The Four of Rods represents the stability of a business or marriage partnership, while the Four of Pentacles stands for financial security.

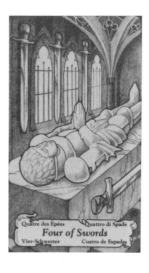

Four of Swords

Four of Cups

Four of Rods

Four of Pentacles

THE FOUR OF SWORDS
(Recuperation)

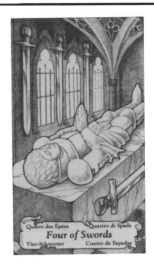

UPRIGHT MEANING: This card shows a knight who has laid down his sword and rests after battle. It signifies a need for inactivity and rest from a physical, emotional, or mental stress that needs healing. Often this card means the client will experience a slow period in his life, which forces him to slow down and rest from conflict. With travel cards in the spread, a vacation might be advisable. Near cards of illness, such as the **Eight of Swords**, the **Star R**, the **Tower**, or the **Ten of Swords**, there is a danger of severe health problems or hospitalization.

SUGGESTED ADVICE: Emphasize the need for rest and recuperation. The client may not have healed completely after a recent illness. Other cards, such as the **Chariot R** or the **Emperor R** may indicate that the client pushes himself and others beyond endurance. He may have a Type A personality and be on the verge of high blood pressure or heart trouble. Encourage him to rest until his full energies have been restored before taking on any more stress.

REVERSED MEANING: This card is a sign that healing and recuperation are complete. The client is ready to resume his former level of activity. With the **Star**, **Strength**, and no Eight, Nine, or Ten of Swords, this card means complete recovery from illness or depression. After a period of inactivity, the level of activity and new interests will increase for the client.

Quatre des Coupe Quattro di Coppe
Four of Cups
Vier-Kelche Cuatro de Copas

THE FOUR OF CUPS (Apathy)

UPRIGHT MEANING: This card shows a man, with three cups, who does not notice a fourth cup offered by a hand from the clouds. The feeling implied by this card is one of boredom, apathy, and dissatisfaction with what one has. The client may feel a bit jaded by the good things he has and uninspired about life. He is ignoring the growth and possibilities symbolized by the fourth cup. The danger is that the client will overlook an opportunity for new inspiration in his life because of a "ho-hum" attitude.

SUGGESTED ADVICE: Notice the cards near the Four of Cups for clues to what is boring and dissatisfying the client. Changes may be necessary in the area shown because it has gone stale for him. Warn the client about the possibility of missed opportunities to regain the joy of life. Ask him what interests, hobbies, people, or activities could excite his interest.

REVERSED MEANING: Here the client sees and is ready to grasp new opportunities, especially in the area of new relationships. He may now see the value of a situation that previously bored him. He is motivated to reach out for the fourth Cup extended from the cloud.

THE FOUR OF RODS
(Partnership)

UPRIGHT MEANING: The four rods on this card symbolize the stability of a permanent, committed relationship. Traditionally, this is the marriage card, but it can also mean a very solid and creative business partnership. The client's creative goals are now in workable, concrete form. He can now see some stability in his life. The energy, enthusiasm, and idealism of the Rods suit can now become concrete and actualized in the life of the client.

SUGGESTED ADVICE: First, explore with the client the possibility of marriage, for this is the primary meaning of the card. If surrounded by good cards, the marriage is favorable. If marriage is unlikely or the client is already married, then a creative goal or a business partnership is very favorable for the client, if other indications in the spread are also favorable.

REVERSED MEANING: In these times, the reversed position can mean non-marital commitment, such as living together. It can also indicate a shaky relationship or marriage and the possibility of dissolving the partnership, if the **Tower** or the **Three of Swords** also appear in the spread. In a business partnership or collaborative effort, there may be a change in creative goals and difference of opinion about business decisions.

Quatre des Deniers   *Quattro di Denari*
Four of Pentacles
Vier-Münzen   *Cuatro de Oros*

THE FOUR OF PENTACLES
(Security)

UPRIGHT MEANING: This card shows a man focusing on a pentacle over his heart, denoting attachment to money and possessions. This card shows a good financial foundation with enough money to cover the basic expenses of life. It indicates a person who is financially stable and secure, with solid investments. This person is very conservative about money and is not inclined to gamble in financial matters. He is very protective of what he has and slowly and steadily increases his net worth through saving money and safe investments. He is self-sufficient both financially and emotionally, for he often equates money with emotional security.

SUGGESTED ADVICE: Although this card shows a practical and financially stable person, it often shows possessiveness and an overly cautious approach to life. The client may be afraid to take risks, both financially and emotionally. He may be trying to be a rock and an island unto himself in exchange for security. The odds are that the client is vaguely unhappy and unfulfilled. Deep down he knows he has sold out for too safe an approach to life.

REVERSED MEANING: Here, the conservatism of the Four of Pentacles has turned to greed and stinginess. The client is haunted by a fear of poverty, which impels him to be grasping and materialistic. He is extremely defensive and self-protective materially and emotionally, fearful of opening up and trusting other people. This card relates to poverty consciousness, no matter how much money the person has. Howard Hughes at the end of his life is a good example of the meaning of this card in the extreme.

Fives

The Five of any suit represents change and instability. With the Sword suit, the instability is caused by betrayal. With Cups, the feeling is one of regret. The Five of Rods represents competition, while the Five of Pentacles stands for insecurity.

Cinq des Epées   Cinque di Spade
Five of Swords
Fünf-Schwerter   Cinco de Espadas

THE FIVE OF SWORDS (Betrayal)

UPRIGHT MEANING: This card shows a gloating and vindictive enemy taking the swords used in battle as the spoils of his victory. It often relates to a betrayal or sneak attack by someone the client trusts and does not suspect to be his enemy. It can refer to an unfaithful lover or a jealous person who sabotages the client behind his back. This card can also relate to vicious gossip and slander. When next to cards relating to the past, such as the **Five of Cups** or the **Six of Cups**, it can mean the client still resents some slight he needs to forgive.

SUGGESTED ADVICE: Since this can be a card of treachery, examine the Court cards in the spread carefully for a clue as to who is working against the client. Warn him that he must be very careful whom he trusts in the near future because his reputation could be hurt by gossip. Tell him that the offending person may be someone he trusts and would not consider a jealous enemy. This could even refer to a past enemy who resurfaces. Advise the client to prepare himself, so that he can minimize the resentment such an attack might provoke.

REVERSED MEANING: The client will be cleared and vindicated of any misunderstanding or gossip. The enemy will be revealed as a vicious troublemaker and no harm will come to the client. This can also refer to the client forgiving past wrongs.

THE FIVE OF CUPS (Regret)

UPRIGHT MEANING: This card depicts a person looking wistfully at three overturned cups while ignoring the two remaining cups. This card pertains to "crying over spilled milk" and pessimism about the future. It often refers to a person who is having difficulty letting go of the past and benefiting from past mistakes. The water spilled from the Cups shows that the cause of regret is more emotional than financial. Often, this card relates to a person who habitually dwells on the past, harboring old grievances. Forgiveness and the ability to recover after emotional loss are necessary. Bitter memories from the past continue to obsess the person. Often a great deal of the blame for past actions is placed on himself.

SUGGESTED ADVICE: Advise the client to let bygones be bygones. Tell him that hindsight is much clearer than foresight and present-day wisdom is gained from the mistakes of the past. If he can understand that all parties involved were doing the best they could with their awareness at the time, he can forgive himself and others.

REVERSED MEANING: The reversed position shows recovery from regret and an acceptance of the past. Now, the person realizes the full implications of the past and appreciates the lessons he learned from the experience. He may even recognize the value of the painful experience in the broader scheme of things in preparing him for later experiences. He is ready to pick up the remaining two Cups that are full of the water of emotional growth and go on.

Cinq des Bâtons Cinque di Bastoni
Five of Rods
Fünf-Stäbe Cinco de Bastos

THE FIVE OF RODS
(Competition)

UPRIGHT MEANING: This card depicts combat and strife, but the rivalry conveyed is not necessarily based on anger. It can represent heated arguments and even physical violence if next to a card of conflict, such as the **Three of Swords**, **Five of Swords**, or **Seven of Swords**. Usually, however, when found next to more neutral cards, the Five of Rods represents the competition necessary to promote a business or an idea. It is the card of "beating the bushes" in order to increase business. When next to Cups or the **Lovers**, it can relate to a suitor's competition for the affections of his sweetheart. Sometimes it relates to a period of struggle to survive in a "dog-eat-dog" situation in business.

SUGGESTED ADVICE: Question the client about feelings of anger and hostility in regards to his situation. If this doesn't strike a chord in him, advise him that his situation calls for an aggressive approach to promoting his own interests. Caution him that a passive "wait and see" attitude could seriously retard his progress at this time.

REVERSED MEANING: This card is like a sigh of relief after conflict and struggle. Now the client can afford to relax his efforts a bit and reap the benefits of his previous promotional efforts. In a more personal sense, he has worked through his anger and hostility and feels more secure in his interpersonal relationships. He doesn't feel he has to be constantly proving himself.

THE FIVE OF PENTACLES
(Insecurity)

UPRIGHT MEANING: Traditionally, this is the card of unemployment. It also relates to freelance work and self-employment because of the financial insecurity often accompanying this type of work. The picture conveys a feeling of being out in the cold, emotionally if not financially. Emotionally, it often relates to a person going through a personal crisis of feeling abandoned or ignored by those close to him. Often, it relates to giving and receiving comfort from another person who is down and out.

SUGGESTED ADVICE: If the person is not literally unemployed, explore with him how he feels about the insecurities of the way he earns his living. His business may be a ''feast or famine'' type of business, causing him to feel he can't really plan ahead. He may have to live hand-to-mouth because of the sporadic nature of his business. If the client has no financial difficulties, this card can mean he doesn't really enjoy his money and feels lonely and neglected by people he cares about. Look for cards in the spread that will help him become closer and more open to other people.

REVERSED MEANING: Here the client is returning to work after a period of unemployment, or his freelance business is picking up after a slow period. It can also mean he feels more secure in his love life and has recovered from a period of emotional insecurity.

Sixes

The Six of any suit represents assistance, idealism, and perfection. With the Sword suit, a change for the better comes through assistance. With Cups, the feeling is one of pleasant memories from the past. The Six of Rods represents triumph, while the Six of Pentacles stands for financial aid.

THE SIX OF SWORDS
(Assistance)

Six des Épées   Sei di Spade
Six of Swords
Sechs-Schwerter   Seis de Espadas

UPRIGHT MEANING: This card shows a man traveling by boat to offer assistance. It represents a turning point for the client. Struggle and strife begin subsiding. Now, problems can be worked out because a "bridge over troubled waters" is extended. This is a time to listen to good advice, to seek help from others, and to learn the lessons of the past by avoiding further turmoil. As the picture suggests, this card can also refer to a trip over water or travel to a place by water.

SUGGESTED ADVICE: When this card appears in a spread, the client has been under stress. The situation now shows signs of improving, although this may not be apparent to him yet. Reassure him that if he listens to the good advice of others and avoids the pitfalls of the past, his worries will soon begin to fade.

REVERSED MEANING: The client may be going "from the frying pan into the fire." On his current course, he is heading into trouble again. He may be ignoring a logical solution to his problems by disallowing others' input. For whatever reason, there is no immediate solution to his problem. This card can also refer to the delay of a trip or the recent return from a trip.

Six des Coupes   Sei di Coppe
Six of Cups
Sechs-Kelche   Seis de Copas

THE SIX OF CUPS (The Past)

UPRIGHT MEANING: The six cups pictured on this card are filled with the flowers of past times. The two children on the card suggest childhood memories. This card usually refers to friends from childhood or friends with whom we have shared pleasant past life experiences. Often, we feel the immediate rapport of karmic ties, as if we had known certain people before. It indicates those people in our life who feel as close as family to us. It is one of the cards that represent children, especially our own. It can indicate the return of a past lover or friend when combined with the **Eight of Cups R** or the **Seven of Swords R**. With the **Six of Pentacles** or the **Empress**, it can represent a gift.

SUGGESTED ADVICE: The cards surrounding this card will indicate whether this is a friend from the past, a karmic tie, or a child. Explore the memories that have been surfacing for the client recently. Perhaps he needs to revisit his childhood home or contact people from his past to get centered in the present and the future.

REVERSED MEANING: This card represents too much attachment to the past and a need to release friends whom the client has outgrown. The client may be looking back nostalgically at an unreal picture of the past, instead of living in the here and now. If he has broken off a love relationship, this card can mean that he is weakening about going back to a past lover, especially if the **Five of Cups** or the **Lovers R** also appears in the spread. Advise him to make his peace with the past and to set his sights on the future.

THE SIX OF RODS (Triumph)

UPRIGHT MEANING: The man on this card carries the wreath of victory as he rides triumphant on his horse. Six rods are raised to honor him. The basic meaning of this card is triumph and realization of goals. The victory often pertains to achieving creative goals in work, arts, or science. This card represents vindication for hard work and struggle to accomplish a cherished dream. The client shows willingness to take a chance on an idea or inspiration and to persist with it to the point of success. With Pentacles, this card indicates business success; with other Rods, the client's ideas will be appreciated. With the **Magician,** the originality of the client could lead him to realize his goals.

SUGGESTED ADVICE: This card in a spread is always a sign of encouragement. Other cards may indicate frustrations and delays, but when this card appears upright, you can assure your client that obstacles to success can be overcome and his efforts will be rewarded. A Major Arcana card next to this card describes the client's probable reaction to attaining his goals.

REVERSED MEANING: This card symbolizes defeat and disillusionment surrounding the client's aspirations. The surrounding cards will indicate whether the rewards are just delayed or denied altogether. When the client is faced with an adversary, such as in a law suit, this card can mean the opponent wins, especially if **Justice R, Judgment R,** or the **Five of Rods** also appear in the spread. If many of the cards in the spread are positive, this card can be a warning not to feel defeated just when success may be within reach.

Six des Deniers   Sei di Denari
Six of Pentacles
Sechs-Münzen   Seis de Oros

THE SIX OF PENTACLES
(Financial Aid)

UPRIGHT MEANING: The picture on this card shows a benefactor, who gives money to those in need of a generous gesture. It often represents good karma in the form of a loan, gift, bonus, grant, or insurance payment. If the **Wheel of Fortune** and the **Sun** also appear in the spread, the money may be unexpected or even unearned, as in a prize won or good luck in gambling. It can indicate extra money available to the client over and above his basic living expenses. It can also indicate a wealthy backer who steps in to ease business expenses. This card often shows the power of the Universe to provide in magical ways for our financial needs.

SUGGESTED ADVICE: The client may not be asking for assistance at a time when it would be available to him. Suggest that he seek out sources of extra money, such as loans, grants, or backers. This is a time of good karma when help is his for the asking, so encourage him to reach out for what is his.

REVERSED MEANING: Now, the pendulum has swung and it is time for the client to pay back loans and grants or any debts that are due. The client may find that extra financial support is withdrawn at this time or a loan or grant may not be renewed. He must tighten his belt and show gratitude for the assistance he has received in the past.

Sevens

The Seven of any suit represents unexpected change, perception, and insight. With the Sword suit, the atmosphere is one of mistrust. With Cups, the insight takes place in the imagination. The Seven of Rods represents a position of advantage, while the Seven of Pentacles stands for a new business perspective.

Sept des Épées — Sette di Spade
Seven of Swords
Sieben-Schwerter — Siete de Espadas

Sept des Coupes — Sette di Coppe
Seven of Cups
Sieben-Kelche — Siete de Copas

Sept des Bâtons — Sette di Bastoni
Seven of Rods
Sieben-Stäbe — Siete de Bastos

Sept des Deniers — Sette di Denari
Seven of Pentacles
Sieben-Münzen — Siete de Oros

Sept des Épées   Sette di Spade
Seven of Swords
Sieben-Schwerter   Siete de Espadas

THE SEVEN OF SWORDS
(Mistrust)

UPRIGHT MEANING: The picture of a man stealthily stealing five of the seven swords shows the traditional meaning of this card as trickery and sneak thievery. The feeling is one of being "ripped off" and victimized by a dishonest person. The treachery can range from insincerity in dealing with people to the intentional duplicity of the con artist. When this card appears with the **Knight of Cups R**, the person it refers to is more phony than actually criminal. When it is near the **Moon R** or the **Five of Swords**, however, beware of actual theft. When Cups, the **Three of Swords**, or the **Five of Swords** also appear in the spread, this can indicate an unfaithful lover.

SUGGESTED ADVICE: Depending on the other cards in the spread, warn the client about possible trickery or "rip off." With difficult cards surrounding, he must be on his guard against underhanded people. If the other cards are predominately favorable, this card can indicate the client is mistrustful and suspicious of people in general. If so, he should examine the reasons for his lack of faith in humanity.

REVERSED MEANING: Here, the client can triumph over the trickery of another and regain what he has lost. This card can indicate the return of stolen property or the return of an unfaithful or unworthy lover who humbly wishes to make restitution. It often represents unexpected triumph after a loss and a feeling that the score has been evened after a victimization.

THE SEVEN OF CUPS
(Imagination)

UPRIGHT MEANING: Each of the seven cups pictured on this card contains a different object, ranging from an octopus to a castle. This card shows emotional identification with many different areas of interest. For this reason, one of its primary meanings is confusion over too many choices and fantasies. With many Cups in the spread, the fantasies usually involve romance, with a glamorized, "rose-colored glasses" approach to love. With the **Star** or the **Magician**, this card can indicate creative talent. Caution the client against possible escapist tendencies through drugs when the **Three of Cups R**, the **Moon**, or **Temperance** also appear with this card.

SUGGESTED ADVICE: The tone of the other cards will indicate whether the client is using his imagination positively or negatively. Even if he is currently daydreaming too much and feeling confused, these negative tendencies can be channeled into a positive use of his imagination, such as painting or writing. Encourage the client to harness his ability to fantasize by using creative visualization or meditation to focus on specific goals.

REVERSED MEANING: Here, the client is willing to set priorities in his life and focus on them. He has overcome the confusion and inertia caused by ambivalence and shows a more realistic attitude toward his idealism and illusions. For people with creative talent, this card can show focused creative goals.

Sept des Bâtons Sette di Bastoni
Seven of Rods
Sieben-Stäbe Siete de Bastos

THE SEVEN OF RODS (Position of Advantage)

UPRIGHT MEANING: At first glance, the man pictured on this card seems overwhelmed by opposing forces. He holds his rod across his chest in a pose of defense against the six rods below him. Because he stands above the opposition, he is in an advantageous position to fight them off. This card indicates the ability to succeed against opposition or competition and to achieve victory through courage. The odds may not be in his favor, but this card shows he can withstand the odds and achieve victory over them. It often refers to being in a position of advantage in business or in any potentially threatening situation.

SUGGESTED ADVICE: When this card is surrounded by favorable cards, the client will fight back successfully and triumph over opposing forces. When cards such as the **Hanged Man** or **Strength R** also appear in the spread, the client may feel weak and defenseless even though he is in a position of advantage. Encourage the client to marshal his forces to keep trying to overcome the threatening circumstances. The odds are that he will surprise himself and come out the victor.

REVERSED MEANING: This is a card of vulnerability, whether real or imagined. The client feels threatened as though he were losing ground. He may be displaying a show of strength but feeling inadequate. Positive cards in the spread will show whether his vulnerability is unwarranted insecurity, while negative cards may indicate that he is fighting a losing battle.

THE SEVEN OF PENTACLES
(New Business Perspective)

Seven of Pentacles

UPRIGHT MEANING: This card shows a man resting after his labor has produced the fruits of seven pentacles. He is tired but now needs to consider new business perspectives. Not only does it show an objective evaluation of one's efforts so far, but also new inspiration about future projects. It sometimes signifies a promotion, a raise, or business travel. It can also mean a good opportunity for a lucrative investment. Money may come in unexpectedly.

SUGGESTED ADVICE: The client has worked hard so far and met with a measure of success, which he should appraise realistically at this time. He may already be thinking of the next step up the ladder or have a new business idea. This should be encouraged to avoid a stale plateau in his career ambitions. Taking financial risks at this time and implementing innovative business changes are likely to bring success.

REVERSED MEANING: An unexpected expense could shake up finances or there could be a shake up at work. The client may have been careless or unmotivated and overlooked errors that will cause problems at work. He may be contemplating a bad business investment or be too undercapitalized to consider investing.

Eights

The Eight of any suit represents control, power, and organization. With the Sword suit, some kind of restriction interferes with the exercise of control or power. With Cups, the client withdraws emotionally from it. The Eight of Rods represents swiftness in all kinds of messages, while the Eight of Pentacles stands for control and power through education.

THE EIGHT OF SWORDS
(Restriction)

Huit des Épées   Otto di Spade
Eight of Swords
Acht-Schwerter   Ocho de Espadas

UPRIGHT MEANING: This card depicts a woman blindfolded, bound by rope, and surrounded by eight vertical swords. The restrictions and severe limitations portrayed here may be external, such as a health problem, or internal, stemming from a self-imposed prison. In many cases, the blindfold implies a lack of understanding of blocks to freedom rather than the reality of the situation. Often a fear of the unknown is connected to the client's refusal to break away from his chains. Major Arcana cards in the spread may help to explain the inner psychological processes at work in the situation. The feeling of frustration and blockage is severe. The client will not be able to ignore the discomfort until he deals with his restrictive situation.

SUGGESTED ADVICE: While surrounding cards may provide clues to the source of the restriction, the client is probably already well aware of the limitations blocking his path. When this card appears, you will hear a lot of ''I can'ts'' and ''Yes, buts'' from the client about breaking free from the problem. Explore with the client his attachments and fears and pay special attention to the timing card (described in the chapter on Reading Spreads). This card can reveal how soon the client may get enough insight to see things more clearly.

REVERSED MEANING: The client sees that his prison is of his own making. He is now ready to act upon this insight. He sees the path to escape and has overcome most of his fear of independence. Encourage the client to step outside of the blocks and restrictions in his life and enjoy his freedom.

Huit des Coupes   Otto di Coppe
Eight of Cups
Acht-Kelche   Ocho de Copas

THE EIGHT OF CUPS
(Withdrawal)

UPRIGHT MEANING: The man on this card has his back turned to the eight cups and appears to be walking away from them. He walks in the direction of the moon rising over a pool of water. The cups, water, and the moon all symbolize an emotional withdrawal of some kind. Often this card refers to a gradual withdrawal of the affections from a relationship. It conveys a feeling of losing interest or backing off and pulling back into oneself emotionally. It is often associated with loneliness but without the intense pain of the **Three of Swords**, because the "handwriting on the wall" has been there for a long time. The situation has been stagnating gradually so that the withdrawal feels more like a shrug of the shoulders than a sudden separation. Usually, the person feels drawn away from the stagnant situation by a more meaningful interest.

SUGGESTED ADVICE: When this card appears in a spread, the client is more than likely aware of diminishing feelings in an existing situation. He may not be able to put his finger on what is now missing from the relationship, but he knows that much of the closeness has left the situation. Advise the client to turn his attention toward those interests that are meaningful to him instead of giving in to the loneliness.

REVERSED MEANING: This card often refers to a person who has trouble with commitment and fears intimacy. He will withdraw and return to the same people and situations periodically. His ambivalence about love causes him to behave in a fickle manner. This card can also represent returning to a situation from which the client withdrew and settling for mediocrity.

THE EIGHT OF RODS (Swiftness)

Eight of Rods

UPRIGHT MEANING: This card shows eight rods flying through the air, signifying air travel and speed. It pertains to good messages of all kinds, whether by phone, mail, or in person. In business matters, it often relates to orders coming in, advertising and promotional efforts paying off, and business picking up. It signifies hope and excitement for achievement of a goal, and is the single most speedy card in the Tarot deck for a quick and encouraging turn of events. When found in the Advice of the Cards section of a spread (see the chapter on Reading Spreads), it can refer to a need for more advertising and promotion to speed up business. In personal matters, this card can signify the arrows of love or love letters coming toward the client. It can also indicate that the client and a lover will become involved and fall in love very quickly.

SUGGESTED ADVICE: If the surrounding cards are favorable, all forms of communication, travel, or advertising in business are beneficial to the client at this time. He will have to live a fast-paced existence to keep up with a stepped-up business schedule. He may need extra help to handle the frenetic pace of business for a while. Since this is a period of "feast" rather than "famine," advise him to take advantage of all opportunities. This card conveys a heady excitement from all the activity and news, and a sense of "too much, too soon" at times.

REVERSED MEANING: Here, we encounter the same frustrations as under Mercury retrograde in astrology: delays of news and travel, and a slowdown in business. The client may feel he is stagnating and vegetating at work, struggling against endless delays, hassles, and miscommunications. He may feel he is perpetually "waiting for Godot" with very few encouraging prospects ahead. Even in personal affairs, this card can signal jealousy occurring in interpersonal relationships. Advise the client to wait this period out until the timing indicates the influence is past. Encourage him to spend his time pursuing projects over which he has total control (such as cleaning closets, writing a book, or arts and crafts).

Huit des Deniers · Otto di Denari
Eight of Pentacles
Acht-Münzen · Ocho de Oros

THE EIGHT OF PENTACLES
(Education)

UPRIGHT MEANING: This card shows a man who eyes a pentacle he can earn. The tools of his trade are on a table before him. This card represents learning a new skill or being trained. It often refers to going to school and gradually learning the necessary skills to earn a living. It is the card of the apprentice rather than the master worker — a person who needs more experience and knowledge in his chosen area of expertise. When the client is working at an established job, this card often pertains to an opportunity to develop a new skill at work. It shows attention to detail and technique and a gradual fine-tuning of an ability until it becomes a skill.

SUGGESTED ADVICE: With Cups, the education can pertain to acquiring relationship skills, perhaps through self-help books or seminars. With Rods, this card can mean learning creative or promotional skills. Encourage the client to pursue classes or training in a new area.

REVERSED MEANING: This card can mean losing interest in a skill or feeling mediocre in a developing area of interest. With students, it can mean losing interest in school or dropping out of school. Often the client is a perfectionist and too critical of himself. Encourage him to persist in his efforts to master the skill rather than giving up because he feels he lacks the necessary talent. If the client works in a field in which he is already skilled, this card can mean he is bored and stagnating. Advise him to seek and devote his energies to a new area of interest.

Nines

The Nine of any suit represents completion and fulfillment. With Swords, the atmosphere is one of worry over the outcome. With Cups, a wish has been fulfilled. The Nine of Rods represents a watch and wait situation, while the Nine of Pentacles stands for a comfortable home.

Neuf des Épées · Nove di Spade
Nine of Swords
Neun-Schwerter · Nueve de Espadas

THE NINE OF SWORDS (Intense Anxiety)

UPRIGHT MEANING: A woman with nine swords over her head sits up in bed, grief-stricken, worried and depressed over worsening problems. She appears riddled with fear and anxiety. Since this is a nine and a high Sword, the situation causing the despair has gone on for some time and has eroded the client's ability to rally. He fears the situation will continue to deteriorate or will never change for the better. The surrounding cards indicate the cause of the anxiety. With Pentacles, the worries are about money, with Cups, emotional matters. With health cards, there is danger of physical or mental breakdown. Often, this card refers to sleepless nights and nightmares provoked by great stress.

SUGGESTED ADVICE: When this card appears, the client must find a solution to the problems preying on his mind. In a case such as severe illness around him, he may need counseling or stress management techniques to handle his distress. In emotional or financial matters, encourage him to seek out creative solutions to his seemingly hopeless troubles before the strain takes its toll on his health.

REVERSED MEANING: This is the "Thank the Lord" card. It shows the release of tension and worry after a long ordeal. The "light at the end of the tunnel" is now in sight and things begin to get better for the client. The client snaps out of the depression and anxiety which have engulfed him for so long.

THE NINE OF CUPS (Wish Fulfillment)

Neuf des Coupes   Nove di Coppe
Nine of Cups
Neun-Kelche   Nueve de Copas

UPRIGHT MEANING: Notice the contented smile in the face of the man on this card. He is happy because something he wished for has come true. Since nine is the number of completion and this is the Cup suit, the fulfillment is often emotional happiness, the fulfillment of a dream. Like the fairy tales about wishes, the duration of this joy depends on how wisely the person chose his wish.

SUGGESTED ADVICE: Although this card is unequivocally good when upright, there is a "catch 22" built into the situation. The client achieves a long cherished dream, only to find that he has grown past those desires. His victory can feel empty. After telling the client things will likely go as he wishes, look for Major Arcana cards in the spread. These may indicate the purpose and significance of the achievement.

REVERSED: Traditionally, this card means the client's wish is delayed or denied. Combined with the **Star**, the **Ten of Cups**, or the **Ten of Pentacles**, it can mean the client has an unrealistic view of his dreams and goals. He may need to visualize and work toward specific priorities to avoid having his wish remain "an impossible dream."

Neuf des Bâtons   Nove di Bastoni
Nine of Rods
Neap-Stäbe   Nueve de Bastos

THE NINE OF RODS (Watch and Wait)

UPRIGHT MEANING: The man pictured on this card wears a bandage around a wound on his head. He stares ahead preparing for further attacks. The man is armed with nine rods should he need to defend himself. This card pertains to a state of readiness and strength in reserve. The situation may require a "wait and see" attitude to properly assess the next course of action. The client will be prepared for the events ahead because he has learned caution and patience from previous experience.

SUGGESTED ADVICE: The client may be very eager to act on a new idea or project. Advise him that his strength lies in waiting out the situation. The ability to wait and see how things develop over time will help him discover the best approach to take for maximum benefit. If the client feels defensive and vulnerable about a new venture, this card assures him he is ready for what comes and adequately prepared to handle the situation.

REVERSED MEANING: The client may impulsively jump into a situation, unprepared for problems that may arise. He may scatter his energies without exercising the necessary patience to let things evolve naturally. This card can also signify a person who is defensive and overly cautious, fearing attack even in safe situations. In this instance, previous wounds and injuries have definitely "gone to his head." The client behaves as if he were in constant battle with the world.

THE NINE OF PENTACLES
(Comfortable Home)

UPRIGHT MEANING: This card shows a woman in her garden with a bird perched on her hand. It conveys enjoyment of animals and nature and the love of a beautiful environment. This card often refers to a person who is well-protected financially. The person has created a home or office environment where he feels harmony and comfort. The Nine of Pentacles can also mean a large financial outlay on the home, real estate, or office improvements. Often, this card depicts solitary affluence and comfort — a person who spends a great deal of time alone.

SUGGESTED ADVICE: The client has created for himself a comfortable and pleasing lifestyle. He should be encouraged to pursue any real estate improvements or investments he may be considering. Redecorating or landscaping plans would be advisable, especially if the **Empress** is also in the spread. Explore the solitary aspect of this card with the client. Is his home a quiet retreat or more of a fortress and hermitage to barricade himself from others?

REVERSED MEANING: This card can mean an upset to the harmony of the home or office. There may be an unexpected repair or expense incurred. The possibility of burglary exists if the **Seven of Swords** or the **Moon** is also present. This card can also indicate a financial loss. The client may have to consider selling a house or moving his office to regroup from this setback.

Tens

The Ten of any suit represents renewal through a new cycle and mastery of lessons regarding the suit in question. With Swords, the cycle ends in disaster. With Cups, love is the outcome. The Ten of Rods represents stress and pressure, while the Ten of Pentacles stands for material prosperity.

THE TEN OF SWORDS (Disaster)

Ten of Swords

UPRIGHT MEANING: This card depicts a man lying face down with ten swords in his back. It signifies utter defeat. The situation in question has failed miserably. There is no choice but to abandon it and start over. This card is actually better than the **Nine of Swords** because the period of anxious waiting and worrying is over. The decision to give up on a losing cause is close at hand. With the **Three of Swords** or the **Four of Rods R**, this card can mean divorce. With the **Ten of Pentacles R** or the **Tower**, it can mean bankruptcy or devastating financial trouble.

SUGGESTED ADVICE: More than likely when this card appears in a client's spread, he is aware that he has a serious problem in the area he asked about. It is best to prepare him for the need to abandon the action that has or will shortly lead him to disaster. The client must consider the best way to recover from a hopeless loss. If he changes his actions now, there is a possibility that his losses will be lessened. Encourage him to try to accept the defeat and to try to understand and learn from his mistakes.

REVERSED MEANING: The client has survived the worst that could happen to him in his situation. Now he must go about the business of getting on his feet again. He must recover and go on, knowing that the disaster he has endured is over and will never be repeated again. The Ten of Swords represents such a crushing blow that even the most foolish die-hard will shrink from repeating his errors. An inner strength and survival instinct are the gifts of having lived through a disastrous Ten of Swords experience. If the client could survive this experience, he has very little left to fear from life. This is a valuable realization.

Dix des Coupes   Dieci di Coppe
Ten of Cups
Zehn-Kelche   Diez de Copas

THE TEN OF CUPS (Love)

UPRIGHT MEANING: This card is reminiscent of the **Two of Cups** with the man and woman facing each other with rapt attention. Instead of two cups, we now have ten cups that form a rainbow, showing that the friendship of the **Two of Cups** has grown into true love. The rapport, compatibility, and intensity of love conveyed in this card is unequaled in the Tarot cards, with the exception of the **Lovers** card. With other favorable cards in the spread, this card indicates the deepest form of mutual love and sharing. With the **Lovers** card or the **Seven of Cups**, the type of love is sexual and romantic, but it can indicate platonic love and very strong friendships without these two cards. With the **Three of Cups**, it can mean a very happy family life. It is the single best card in the Tarot deck for happiness in personal relationships.

SUGGESTED ADVICE: The cards surrounding the Ten of Cups will describe the type of love and the people with whom the client feels this harmony and sharing. Advise the client to draw upon the support and love of those people who truly care for him. This card is a ''pat on the back'' from the Tarot, indicating that the client not only knows how to receive love but also how to give it.

REVERSED MEANING: The perfect relationship described above has some snags. There may be arguments and disharmony obstructing the usual flow of the relationship. Areas of incompatibility may be surfacing. One of the parties may not feel as committed or as ''in love'' as the other. The client will have to work out some problems before the rapport can return to the high level of previous sharing.

THE TEN OF RODS (Stress and Pressure)

UPRIGHT MEANING: This card shows a man struggling under the weight of ten rods he is carrying in his arms. He looks down as he walks, unable to shift the burden so he can look up at the sky. This symbolizes the strain and pressure on the client's shoulders. The heavy burden often relates to a workaholic, "all work and no play" personality. This person takes on more responsibility than he should and often lacks the ability to delegate work. His attitude is the proverbial "If you want something done right, you have to do it yourself."

SUGGESTED ADVICE: The client has let his real or imagined responsibilities overshadow the joyful, playful side of life, to the extent that his life has become a drudge. With the **Emperor R** or the **Magician R**, the client may be abusing his power and behaving like a tyrant. With the **Five of Swords** or the **Seven of Swords**, he most likely resents the extra work that he does, and feels like a martyr. Suggest ways that he can learn to relax, enjoy life, and be more balanced in his approach to work. Hiring an extra employee or taking a vacation may be in order. The message of this card is to lighten up.

REVERSED MEANING: This card is like a huge sigh of relief because the pressure is off. With positive cards, some event may have removed the feeling of stress and strain the client has been under. More likely, however, the client has learned some lessons about worrying and feeling crushed by responsibility. He has allowed himself to view life with more joy and optimism. He has finally shifted his burden so he can once more see the sky.

Ten of Pentacles

THE TEN OF PENTACLES
(Material Prosperity)

UPRIGHT MEANING: This card shows a man and a woman, and an old man holding a dog and a child. Behind them is a castle. It conveys a sense of happiness and contentment beyond financial riches. This is because the security comes from a family group or a corporate group. It can indicate a windfall from an inheritance, stocks, or other investments. The degree of financial prosperity depends on the client's situation and his view of what constitutes a large increase in money. Obviously, this will vary considerably for a rich man or a poor man. This card can also relate to large purchases, such as a house or land, or big business deals involving millions of dollars.

SUGGESTED ADVICE: When this card appears in a spread, the client is probably already very financially secure or working in that direction. When this card is surrounded by good cards, advise the client to expand his holdings, and to use any large sums of money that come his way to further his success and security.

REVERSED: This card is a warning of heavy losses in investments or trouble over inheritance. The client may be forced to sell a house or land to recover from financial difficulties. His corporation may be in serious financial straits. The client must regroup and drastically restructure finances in order to survive.

The Court Cards

Overview

The Court Cards correspond to the face cards in an ordinary deck. They usually represent people in our lives rather than situations or events.

- The **Pages** can represent either messages or young people up to the age of 25, of either sex.

- The **Knights** represent men between the ages of 25 and 40.

- The **Queens** signify women over the age of 25.

- The **Kings** deal with men over the age of 40.

When a Court Card appears in a spread, you can try to determine who that card stands for by associating its suit with physical appearance or astrological sign.

The suits tell us the hair and eye coloring of the Court cards.

- The coloring for Swords is medium-brown hair and light eyes. For example, the Page of Swords is a medium-brown haired, light-eyed child under age 25. The Knight of Swords is a medium-brown haired, light-eyed man between ages 25 and 40. The Queen of Swords is a woman over age 25 with medium-brown hair and light eyes. The King of Swords is a medium-brown haired man, with light eyes, over age 40.

- The coloring for **Cups** is blond or gray hair and light eyes.

- The coloring for **Rods** is sandy or reddish hair, light or freckled skin, and dark or light eyes.

- The coloring for **Pentacles** is dark hair, skin, and eyes. This suit can represent blacks or other dark-skinned ethnic groups.

The four suits of the Minor Arcana can also be related to the earth, air, fire, and water signs in astrology.

- The **Swords** correspond to the air signs which are Gemini, Libra, and Aquarius. When reading a Sword Court Card, you might want to describe the person astrologically as an air sign to further define the person in the spread.

- The **Cups** correspond to the water signs in astrology which are Cancer, Scorpio, and Pisces.

- The **Rods** correspond to the fire signs which are Aries, Leo, and Sagittarius.

- The **Pentacles** correspond to the earth signs which are Taurus, Virgo, and Capricorn.

This means that when you are describing a person who is represented in the cards, for example, by the Knight of Swords, your description would include not only that he is brown-haired and light-eyed, but that his astrological sign may be Gemini, Libra, or Aquarius. In cases where the two conflict, you may need to choose between physical appearance and astrological sign when describing the person.

To summarize:

Ages of Court Cards

Page - young person of either sex, aged 0-25

Knight - man aged 25-40

Queen - woman over 25

King - man over 40

Coloring of Suits

Swords - brown hair and light eyes

Cups - blonde or gray hair and light eyes

Rods - sandy or reddish hair

Pentacles - dark hair, eyes, and skin (blacks or foreigners)

Astrological Signs of Suits

Swords - air signs (Gemini, Libra, Aquarius)

Cups - water signs (Cancer, Scorpio, Pisces)

Rods - fire signs (Aries, Leo, Sagittarius)

Pentacles - earth signs (Taurus, Virgo, Capricorn)

Pages

The Page of any suit represents either a message or a young person under the age of 25. With the Sword suit, the message is one of forceful communication. With Cups, the message is social. The Page of Rods represents an enthusiastic message, while the Page of Pentacles is a message about financial dealings.

Valet des Épées   Fante di Spade
Page of Swords
Schwerter-Bube   Sota de Espadas

THE PAGE OF SWORDS
(Forceful Communication)

UPRIGHT MEANING: The Page of Swords refers to direct and outspoken communication in which a person "calls a spade a spade." It shows intelligence and assertiveness in the use of words, such as a lawyer would use defending a case. The message conveyed may be upsetting and blunt, but there can be very little doubt about the meaning intended. Sometimes, this card refers to a legal summons or constructive criticism, which may be upsetting but also clears the air about an issue. Since the Sword suit deals with the air signs in astrology, this card can also refer to a young person under the age of 25, who is a Gemini, Libra, or Aquarius. His or her coloring would be brown hair and light eyes. The person would possess a mental orientation toward life.

SUGGESTED ADVICE: If this card does not refer to the person described above, the issue may be the need to speak plainly about a very delicate or upsetting issue. The question posed and the other cards in the spread may indicate the area of possible turmoil. Emphasize the benefits of an honest and open heart-to-heart talk to resolve the issue.

REVERSED MEANING: There is a danger here of a serious misunderstanding, because of a critical and harsh way of communicating ideas. Angry and defensive exchanges are likely, if the client doesn't back off and see things objectively before speaking. If this card refers to a young person, he may be hostile and belligerent toward the client. The client will encounter great resistance in trying to discuss matters with the young person until his grievances have been aired.

THE PAGE OF CUPS (Social Messages)

UPRIGHT MEANING: The young person pictured on this card gazes intently at a fish appearing out of a cup or chalice. The fish, a creature that lives in water, symbolizes the life brought forth from warm, open communications between people. This card can indicate pleasant letters, phone calls, or social invitations when it appears near the **Two of Cups**, **Three of Cups**, or other Pages. With family cards such as the **Four of Rods,** the **Ten of Pentacles,** or the **Six of Cups,** this card would more likely refer to a child in the client's life. This card traditionally has been associated with gay people, but the meaning should obviously be reserved for special circumstances where you feel you can speak candidly with the client.

SUGGESTED ADVICE: Based on the tone of the other cards in the spread, determine first if the Page refers to a message about social affairs or a person in the client's life. If this card refers to a young person under the age of 25, his coloring would be light hair and eyes and his temperament would be sensitive and emotional (Cancer, Scorpio, or Pisces). The client's dealings with this person could challenge both of them to be open and honest about their feelings. If this card refers to social communications, it would be beneficial for the client to phone, write, or otherwise extend social invitations.

REVERSED MEANING: This card can signify a slow period in social affairs, when the client is not likely to hear from friends or be invited out frequently. It can also signify that the client prefers to slow down on his social activities for a time and spend more time alone.

Valet des Bâtons   Fante di Bastoni
Page of Rods
Stäbe-Bube   Sota de Bastos

THE PAGE OF RODS
(Enthusiasm)

UPRIGHT MEANING: The Page of Rods is a card of exciting, energetic messages. It often refers to good news. It may also relate to a young person under the age of 25, who is sandy or reddish haired with dark or light eyes. The young person would be a fire temperament (Aries, Leo, or Sagittarius) and would be enterprising and creative by nature. He or she may be a bit impulsive and quick to react but has a winning and dynamic personality. This young person needs an active and athletic life to make use of his high energy level.

SUGGESTED ADVICE: This card may refer to the client or a young person around the client who is lively and enterprising. This card can also mean that the client will soon hear good news. Combined with Cups, the good news would concern emotional matters. With Pentacles, the good news would relate to finances. Since the Pages are communications cards, the client may be very excited about an idea and communicate his thoughts in an inspiring and enthusiastic way.

REVERSED MEANING: The young person referred to above may be flighty, scatterbrained, or over-reactive. His desire for instant results may make him rash and testy. The client may hear some bad news or communicate his ideas hastily and insensitively.

THE PAGE OF PENTACLES
(Financial Dealings)

UPRIGHT MEANING: The Page of Pentacles represents all kinds of communications about money. These can include contracts, negotiations, and all forms of "wheeling and dealing" involved in commerce. It can mean good messages regarding doing business with new clients or launching new business ventures. It involves all forms of conversation, letters, or discussions that enhance business relationships. This card refers to a no-nonsense, down-to-earth type of communication. Since the Pentacle suit deals with the earth signs in astrology, this card can also refer to a young person under the age of 25, who is a Taurus, Virgo, or Capricorn. He or she would be dark-haired, dark-eyed, and very conscientious in studies and financial affairs.

SUGGESTED ADVICE: If the card is not describing an actual person in the client's life, the indication is positive for business negotiations or even contracts. This is especially true if the **Justice** or **Judgment** card also appears in the spread. If the client actively engages in calling or seeing business contacts at this time, he can arrive at some beneficial agreements.

REVERSED MEANING: This can mean delays in communicating with key business contacts. News about money matters may be disappointing, or the client may need to be careful not to waste money now. If this card describes a young person in the client's life, the person may be very self-critical and insecure about his scholastic or financial abilities.

Knights

The Knight of any suit represents a man between the ages of 25 and 40. With the Sword suit, the person is assertive, and possibly an air sign with medium hair and light eyes. With Cups, the person is congenial, and may be a water sign with blond or gray hair and light eyes. The Knight of Rods is an energetic, fire sign person with sandy or reddish hair, while the Knight of Pentacles is a shrewd, earth sign person with dark hair, eyes, and skin.

Cavalier des Epées   Cavaliere di Spade
Knight of Swords
Schwerter-Ritter   Caballo de Espadas

Cavalier des Coupes   Cavaliere di Coppe
Knight of Cups
Kelche-Ritter   Caballo de Copas

Cavalier des Bâtons   Cavaliere di Bastoni
Knight of Rods
Stäbe-Ritter   Caballo de Bastos

Cavalier des Deniers   Cavaliere di Denari
Knight of Pentacles
Münzen-Ritter   Caballo de Oros

THE KNIGHT OF SWORDS
(Assertive Action)

Cavalier des Epées   Cavaliere di Spade
Knight of Swords
Schwerter-Ritter   Caballo de Espadas

UPRIGHT MEANING: The Knight wields his sword courageously and charges forward with the force of his intellect. This card often refers to a situation that calls for a mental rather than a physical show of strength. The client may need to act on his strong opinions rather than simply talking the issue to death. This card can also refer to a young man between 25 and 40, who is brown-haired and light-eyed. He is an air sign type (Gemini, Libra, or Aquarius) with a sharp mind and love of mental challenge.

SUGGESTED ADVICE: The surrounding cards will give clues to the type of situation calling for assertive action. For example, Pentacles denote money issues while Cups involve emotional issues. If this card does not signify the client himself, it represents a person who can stimulate the client to act forcefully on his beliefs and thoughts. The Knight of Swords is very confrontative and mentally direct. He may spark resolve on the part of the client to stand up for himself intellectually.

REVERSED MEANING: This card can represent the sledgehammer approach to pressing a point. It shows the use of too much force and energy to assert a stand. The client may feel angry or defensive and overstate his case or act recklessly. He would be seen as hostile and sarcastic or fanatical and potentially violent in his actions. This card shows a temporary loss of objectivity and good judgment. Warn the client not to act until he has put his thoughts back in perspective. If this card represents another person, he is likely to be a pushy, aggressive troublemaker whom the client would do well to avoid.

Cavalier des Coupes   Cavaliere di Coppe
Knight of Cups
Kelche-Ritter   Caballo de Copas

THE KNIGHT OF CUPS
(Congeniality)

UPRIGHT MEANING: The Knight of Cups represents a young man between the ages of 25 and 40, who is popular because of his pleasant personality. He has a lot of natural charm and may be considered a "ladies' man." He is sensitive, emotionally warm, and a good listener. He enjoys interacting with people and does well in sales, counseling, or personnel work. His coloring is light hair and light eyes and his astrological sign may be Cancer, Scorpio, or Pisces. Usually, this card refers to a person, but it may also mean social invitations.

SUGGESTED ADVICE: If this card does not relate to the client himself, it represents someone around the client who is very astute at handling people. He may benefit the client as a friend or as a business associate through his winning personality and emotional sensitivity. In a woman's reading, this card can refer to social invitations from a romantic interest in her life.

REVERSED MEANING: When he is reversed, the Knight is still charming but in a manipulative and insincere way. He is likable on the surface, but is superficial and lacks genuineness. With women, this man is a Don Juan who uses women with a "love 'em and leave 'em" attitude. This is the Dance-Away Lover who fears emotional commitment and depth.

THE KNIGHT OF RODS (Energy)

Cavalier des Bâtons   Cavaliere di Bastoni
Knight of Rods
Stäbe-Ritter   Caballo de Bastos

UPRIGHT MEANING: The Knight of Rods is a card of dynamic energy and movement.   In combination with other cards, such as the **Eight of Rods**, the **Six of Swords**, the **Fool**, the **World**, or the **Wheel of Fortune**, it can mean travel.   When combined with the **Tower**, the **Four of Rods R**, or the **Nine of Pentacles R**, it can refer to a change of residence.   Since it is a Court card, it also can relate to a young man of fiery temperament (Aries, Leo, or Sagittarius) between 25 and 40, who is ardent and hasty by nature.   He is a high-energy person who loves spur-of-the-moment decisions and actions. He may be quite athletic and enjoy dangerous and adventurous enterprises. He tends to have sandy or reddish hair, freckled skin, and light or dark eyes.

SUGGESTED ADVICE: Look for the card combinations listed above for possible travel or change of residence. If the description of the person above does not fit the client, advise the client that a very dynamic and energetic young man will be involved in his question. This person could help the client interject new enthusiasm into his life.

REVERSED MEANING: This card can refer to a delay of travel or a change of residence, if other combination cards are present in the spread. If the card relates to an actual person, he will be pushy, unreliable, inconsistent, and impatient. He may represent a jealous and demanding lover.

Cavalier des Deniers   Cavaliere di Denari
Knight of Pentacles
Münzen-Ritter   Caballo de Oros

THE KNIGHT OF PENTACLES
(Shrewd Business Activities)

UPRIGHT MEANING: The Knight of Pentacles usually represents a dark-haired, dark-eyed man between 25 and 40 with a practical and business-oriented temperament (Taurus, Virgo, Capricorn). He knows how to spot and capitalize on opportunities to make money. His motives and actions are based on a strong need for security and responsibility in his life. He is not afraid of hard work and is persistent in reaching his goals. He is more concerned with the HOW TO of life rather than the WHY. He can be very particular about how he spends his money, often preferring to save it until he is sure of a safe investment. When this card does not refer to a person, it represents action taken in business affairs and the exchange of money.

SUGGESTED ADVICE: If this card does not represent the client, it may represent a very reliable and responsible suitor for a woman client. For a male client, this man may be a valuable friend or business associate because of his patience, practicality and loyalty. His judgment in business matters would always be based on common sense and potential profit. He would be a good provider and a conscientious employee.

REVERSED MEANING: Here, the Knight is all work and no play, with a tendency to ignore other aspects of his life in favor of a workaholic lifestyle. He may be caught up in meaningless rituals and unproductive routines in his work, and be unwilling to try more efficient methods. He tends to worry too much about money and can be miserly in his spending habits. He is critical of other people's mistakes but blind to his own. When this card does not refer to a person, it indicates a slowdown or delay in business matters or finances.

Queens

The Queen of any suit represents a woman over the age of 25. With the Sword suit, the person is strong-willed, and possibly an air sign with medium-brown hair and light eyes. With Cups, the person is nurturing, and may be a water sign with blond or gray hair and light eyes. The Queen of Rods is an exuberant, fire sign person with sandy or reddish hair, while the Queen of Pentacles is a practical, earth sign person with dark hair, eyes, and skin.

Reine des Epées — Regina di Spade
Queen of Swords
Schwerter-Königin — Reina de Espadas

THE QUEEN OF SWORDS
(Strong-Willed)

UPRIGHT MEANING: Traditionally, the Queen of Swords refers to a widow or divorced woman because of her strength and take-charge attitude. She is a contradiction in terms: though pictured as a very feminine woman, she is armed with a sword as if to do battle. Her stern and no-nonsense demeanor is reminiscent of Joan of Arc. Because she is of the Sword suit, her intellect and intelligence are forces with which to contend. Her sword is often a sharp tongue. She demands and expects to be treated as an equal, having proven herself equal to the task of coping with life's trials. She may appear dominating and intimidating to men because she prefers to wear a tough exterior and does not show her fragility easily. Often highly educated or very bright, she needs a man who appreciates her mental accomplishments and strong will. Her coloring may be brown hair and light eyes and her astrological sign may be Gemini, Libra, or Aquarius.

SUGGESTED ADVICE: This card may describe the client herself or a person around the client. If this card represents a friend, she will be helpful in sharing her strength and determination with the client. Her tenacity in overcoming obstacles will be an inspiration to less hardy souls. If this card represents a romantic interest of the client, advise him to overcome his intimidation. By getting to know her, he can uncover the tenderness and fragility within every Queen of Swords.

REVERSED MEANING: This card can represent a demanding and brow-beating woman. Usually, she has become embittered by past hardships. She turns her resentment towards other people in the form of vindictive, jealous, and petty behavior. She is pushy and defensive with men and untrusting and jealous of other women. She needs to re-evaluate her assumptions and attitudes about life.

THE QUEEN OF CUPS
(Nurturing)

UPRIGHT MEANING: The Queen of Cups and the Empress are the traditional cards of the mother, representing a caring and emotional woman over the age of 25. The Queen holds her cup filled with gentleness and kindness for others to drink from. She understands intuitively the emotional needs of others and is usually a good listener and counselor. She is a romantic person, believing idealistically that love is the answer to life's problems. She believes in giving people the benefit of the doubt and enjoys helping others. Her sweet and forgiving nature makes her a favorite with other people. She is light-haired or gray-haired with light eyes. Her astrological sign may be Cancer, Scorpio, or Pisces.

SUGGESTED ADVICE: If this card does not represent the client, advise the client to draw upon the emotional sensitivity of this motherly, caring person around him. She may be his own mother or a friend who is very kind and helpful. Especially in emotional issues, he will gain insight and good advice from a heart-to-heart talk with the Queen of Cups. This kind of woman often makes a good lover, wife, and mother and could be the kind of woman a male client needs in his love life.

REVERSED MEANING: Here, the Queen of Cups is over-emotional and too easily influenced by sentiment. She is naive and vulnerable, often gullible. She is a sucker for a sob story and may be used mercilessly by manipulative people. She is friendly but superficial in her dealing with others. Her lack of good judgment and discrimination makes her easy prey for any hard luck story, without regard to how deserving the other person is of help and assistance. She does not draw upon her instinctive feelings about people, but becomes the surrogate mother for any and all.

Reine des Bâtons   Regina di Bastoni
Queen of Rods
Stäbe-Königin   Reina de Bastos

THE QUEEN OF RODS
(Exuberance)

UPRIGHT MEANING: The woman that this card describes is a fire sign personality (Aries, Leo, Sagittarius) who shows independence and a spirited creativity. She is ardent in love and shows her feelings openly. She becomes enthusiastic about new ideas and is dynamic and enterprising in business. She has a bubbly and outgoing personality and sparkles with vivacity in social situations. Because she is a Rod, she would have sandy or reddish hair and fair, freckled skin. Her eyes could be light or dark. She is over 25 years old.

SUGGESTED ADVICE: This card may describe the client or an important person pertaining to the client's question. Whether he currently knows her or not, the above description will give him enough information to recognize the Queen of Rods when she enters his life. If she is surrounded by favorable cards, her influence will be creative and she will inspire the client with her enthusiasm.

REVERSED MEANING: This card describes a woman who is creative but scatters her energies through disorganization. She may appear flighty or scatterbrained and always seems to be running late. She is rather long-winded in conversation but is a poor listener. She is high-strung and may become hysterical under pressure. She is prone to over-emotionalism and is likely to cry or fly off the handle easily.

THE QUEEN OF PENTACLES
(Practicality)

Queen of Pentacles

UPRIGHT MEANING: The woman on this card holds a rabbit and a pentacle. She represents an earth sign woman (Taurus, Virgo, or Capricorn) who is very down-to-earth and resourceful in business. She is well organized and ambitious to succeed financially, and is an asset to any business setting. She is a go-getter whose instincts in business are excellent and will take her a long way. She is over 25 years of age and her coloring is dark hair and eyes. Practical considerations rule her heart and she is unlikely to be swayed much by sentimentality.

SUGGESTED ADVICE: This card may represent the client or an important person in the situation. The client may do well to listen to her sound practical suggestions about the issue in question. She would make an excellent employee or organizer because of her considerable business ability.

REVERSED MEANING: This woman's values are very materialistic and superficial. She is the status-seeker and gold-digger *par excellence*, driven to value herself and others based on prestige and labels on clothes. Her tendency to name-drop shows the underlying insecurity and feelings of inferiority in her personality.

Kings

The King of any suit represents a man over 40. With the Sword suit, the person is intelligent, and possibly an air sign with medium-brown hair and light eyes. With Cups, the person is protective, and may be a water sign with blond or gray hair and light eyes. The King of Rods is a creative, fire sign person with sandy or reddish hair, while the King of Pentacles possesses business ability and is an earth sign person with dark hair, eyes, and skin.

THE KING OF SWORDS
(Intelligence)

Roi des Épées   Re di Spade
King of Swords
Schwerter-König   Rex de Espada

UPRIGHT MEANING: The King of Swords carries the sword of intellect with dignity and confidence. He has developed and fine-tuned his mind to a high degree. He is often an educated man who makes his living through his intellect, such as a doctor or lawyer. He possesses good verbal skills and a quick wit. His gift of repartee serves him well in his chosen profession. He is curious about many subjects and enjoys learning for its own sake. He is very perceptive and bright, enjoying lively conversations and mental battles. He is not a person to cross because he will go for the jugular to win his point. He is over 40 with dark hair that may be graying and light eyes. Since he is a Sword, his astrological sign may be Gemini, Libra, or Aquarius.

SUGGESTED ADVICE: The person described above may refer to the client or one of his associates. In medical or legal situations, this card often represents the doctor or lawyer. His curiosity and brilliant intellect will sharpen the client's wits in personal or business associations.

REVERSED MEANING: Here, the King of Swords has degenerated into a verbal manipulator, who may be ruthless for power. He can be harsh and merciless and use people heartlessly. He is a person who uses his mental abilities selfishly to coerce others to bend to his will. He can be cruel and unfeeling in personal relationships. He may mistrust other people and treat them with the calculating strategy of a chess player in his dealings with them.

Roi des Coupes — Re di Coppe
King of Cups
Kelche-König — Rey de Copas

THE KING OF CUPS (Protective)

UPRIGHT MEANING: The King of Cups holds a cup, which symbolizes his emotional openness. He is kind and sensitive. Often, he is a family man who is very nurturing and protective toward his children. He may be employed in the helping professions, such as the ministry or counseling, because he enjoys helping people and listening to their problems. He is over 40, with light or gray hair and light eyes. Since he is a Cup, his astrological sign may be Cancer, Scorpio, or Pisces.

SUGGESTED ADVICE: If this card does not represent the client, it may refer to the client's father. The **Emperor** or King of Cups often relates to the person's father. It can also mean a very fatherly person in whom the client can confide. His emotional sensitivity would make him a good choice for a friend.

REVERSED MEANING: This man has gone overboard emotionally, in the sense that he lacks balance between the thinking and feeling sides of his personality. He tends to smother and spoil his loved ones, and to encourage dependency through overprotectiveness. He has difficulty letting go of destructive relationships in his life. He may be a heavy drinker who becomes maudlin and sentimental under the influence of alcohol.

THE KING OF RODS
(Entrepreneur)

Roi des Bâtons   Re di Bastoni
King of Rods
Stäbe-König   Rey de Bastos

UPRIGHT MEANING: The King of Rods represents a creative man of vision. He is a dynamic self-starter with boundless energy, unafraid to take risks or speculate to achieve his goals. He is open to new ideas and enjoys promoting them with enthusiasm. Often, he is a self-made man who works independently. You may also find him working in the fields of sales, marketing, promotion, or advertising, since he can motivate others and enjoys inspiring them to live up to their potential. He is over 40 with sandy or reddish hair and light or dark eyes. Because he is a Rod, his astrological sign may be Aries, Leo, or Sagittarius.

SUGGESTED ADVICE: If this card refers to the client, encourage him to use his vision and creativity. If this is a person around him, he will be an inspiring, motivating force in the client's life. His energy and dynamism can spark new ideas. He infects those around him with excitement and hope. This optimism and willingness to gamble is contagious.

REVERSED MEANING: This man is impulsive and impatient in business decisions. He is still a promoter, but more of the con artist variety. He often gets involved in get-rich-quick schemes. He latches onto scheme after scheme with high hopes and enthusiasm, only to be disappointed or lack the patience to wait for success. He has a quick temper and can be temperamental in other ways as well.

Roi des Deniers — Re di Denari
King of Pentacles
Münzen-König — Rey de Oros

THE KING OF PENTACLES
(Business Ability)

UPRIGHT MEANING: The King of Pentacles represents a mature man over 40 who is very astute in business matters. He is often a banker, stockbroker, merchant, or realtor by profession. He understands the workings of the business world and is comfortable with the everyday demands of commerce. Often, he is a man of means because of his innate practicality and reliability in financial matters. His mathematical and accounting ability help him rise to a level of authority in his chosen business. Because he is a Pentacle, he is dark-haired and dark-eyed and of the earth temperament (Taurus, Virgo, or Capricorn).

SUGGESTED ADVICE: If this card does not refer to the client himself, it represents a very sharp business contact who may be helpful to the client in practical matters. His advice in financial matters or business would be sound and knowledgeable. As a romantic partner, the King of Pentacles would be loyal, dependable, and financially stable.

REVERSED MEANING: This man is very money oriented and very desirous of success, but either lacks business sense or doesn't use his abilities well. He is often wasteful and disorganized, mismanaging what resources he has. He may be a wheeler-dealer in business, expecting to get rich without putting in the planning and conscientiousness necessary for success.

The Major Arcana

Overview

The Major Arcana cards carry the deepest symbolic meaning of the Tarot deck. This symbolic quality can best be compared to the metaphors used in poetry. Each Major Arcana card represents a distinct step in the psychological and spiritual evolution of mankind. In a reading, the Major Arcana cards usually refer to psychological attitudes, lessons, and super levels of awareness rather than to everyday events. However, some of the characters in the Major Arcana such as the Fool, High Priestess, Emperor, Empress and others can represent important people in your life.

The best way to approach the Major Arcana is to reach beyond the standard meaning of each card and associate it intuitively with feelings, experiences, literature, or drama. This process of associating freely with the *soul* of each card personalizes it in your own frame of reference and stimulates the intuition.

For example, the Fool might conjure up the playful innocence of Puck in *A Midsummer Night's Dream* or Peter Pan who refused to grow up. Without these personal associations, you might be limited to an abstract intellectual approach to the Fool's naivete and playfulness. With personal associations to the energy of the Fool, he is no longer a stilted wooden figure, but comes to life like Pinocchio and expresses his own unique vitality in action. It is like the difference between a slide and a movie when each Tarot figure comes to life in your own imagination.

Meanings of the Major Arcana Cards

There are 22 cards in the Major Arcana, beginning with the Fool numbered 0 and progressing in consecutive order up to the World numbered XXI. Their upright and reversed meanings are summarized as follows for quick reference.

0 Fool   naive; fresh, innocent approach; optimism; willing to take a chance

Reversed   too idealistic; Pollyanna; risky, foolish move; foolhardy

I Magician	enterprising, resourceful, inventive, intuitive ideas; independent strong-willed man; streak of genius
Reversed	inconsistent; erratic; unstable; rebellious; self-willed; headstrong; man who is domineering; commitment phobia
II High Priestess	hidden powers; deep mystery; woman who is intriguing, reserved and secretive; inscrutable older woman
Reversed	intentional intrigue and secrecy; misuse of psychic powers; spying; not looking deep enough
III Empress	comfort; luxury; ease; generosity; abundance; the mother; prosperity; fertility
Reversed	laziness; excess; extravagance; promiscuity; hedonism; spoils other people
IV Emperor	father figure; authority; final decision maker; boss; law and order
Reversed	tyrant; egomaniac; arbitrary in decisions; domineering
V Hierophant	society's rules; rigid; dogmatic; in a rut; hidebound; mindless tradition; status quo; conventional; orthodox religion
Reversed	ready to break out of a rut; open to innovative, unconventional ideas
VI Lovers	relationship based on intense attraction; passion; karmic tie; choosing correct path
Reversed	jealous, possessive, devouring love; obsessive, immature reactions in love; destructive passion; choosing wrong path
VII Chariot	action; assertiveness; will power; drive and ambition; new car; trip
Reversed	reckless action; no respect for law and order; misuse of power; stepping on people on the way to the top; car trouble; scattered energy

VIII Strength	quiet confidence and self-reliance; ability to cope; good health
Reversed	show of strength with fear and insecurity behind it; fear of failure; physically drained
IX Hermit	serious; reclusive; introverted; spartan; discipline; teacher; study; inner guidance and wisdom
Reversed	paranoid; afraid of close relationships; too withdrawn; "I am a rock, I am an island"
X Wheel of Fortune	good luck; "synchronicity"; coincidence; sudden events
Reversed	bad luck; Murphy's law; "one thing after another"; petty annoyances; minor setbacks; ups and downs
XI Justice	karmic or legal justice; balanced judgment; appropriate resolution
Reversed	injustice; prejudice; bias; illegal activity; out of balance; wasted energy; overcompensation
XII Hanged Man	self-sacrifice; suspension; on hold; ambivalence; biding your time
Reversed	ready for decision and action; life is off hold; "all systems go"
XIII Death	endings and beginnings; cooperating in reevaluation and revamping of situation
Reversed	resisting change and needed transformation; holding on to decaying conditions; forced change
XIV Temperance	here and now awareness; appropriate action; zen-like gift for diplomacy and timing; controlling eating, drinking, smoking, dieting, or spending
Reversed	impulsive; overreaction; poor sense of timing; no flow; out of sync; going on a binge
XV Devil	temptation; settling for safe, comfortable, easy situation but no growth; giving in to a weakness; backsliding; choosing a situation for the wrong reasons
Reversed	overcoming a weakness or temptation; overcoming inertia and stagnation

XVI Tower	plans fall apart; breakdown of false structure; false sense of security crumbles; unexpected shakeup in plans; surprising turn of events
Reversed	releasing a past mistake; acceptance of the necessary collapse of false security
XVII Star	dreams; meditation; visualization; optimism; sense of purpose; inspiring wishes and dreams; vision and hope for one's highest potential
Reversed	disillusionment; hopelessness; depression; pessimism; purposelessness; illness
XVIII Moon	psychic ability; dreams; behind the scene activity; unspoken messages; more than meets the eye
Reversed	subversive activity; psychic attack; sabotage; rip off; drugs; illegal acts; hidden things come to light; misunderstandings; being secretly undermined; bad vibrations
XIX Sun	honor; recognition; fulfillment of goals; success
Reversed	too much ego; showy; wanting to be center stage; content to look good but not earn success; pessimism; negativity; failure
XX Judgment	good karma; winning law suit; beginning of new cycle; reward for positive effect; reap what you have sown
Reversed	negative karma; losing law suit; punishment for failure to learn; still more lessons to learn; bad judgment
XXI World	mastery over a situation or field; international travel; able to handle all aspects well; completion; synthesis
Reversed	limited understanding of the situation; not seeing total picture; unfinished business; almost ready for completion and a new cycle

0 THE FOOL (Innocence)

0 Le Fou   0 Il Matto
0 The Fool
0 Der Narr   0 El Loco

UPRIGHT MEANING: The Fool is numbered 0 in the Tarot deck because he represents both the beginning and culmination of the experiences each person encounters in his quest for awareness. As the neophyte beginning the journey through the experiences symbolized by the 21 other Major Arcana cards, he is youthful and childlike. He is exuberant in his willingness to take chances, and experiences life with naive optimism. He does not linger long in any one experience. He prefers to live in the moment and enjoy the here and now. For this reason, he may prefer the lifestyle of the vagabond or wanderer, avoiding responsibility for his actions. He chooses to remain aloof from the entrapping games of society. He may back away from situations involving depth and intensity. He is inexperienced, but relies on his instincts and intuitions to protect him. Without further awareness, the Fool would be content merely to skim the surface of life. He most likely would be forced to learn from his foolhardiness and naivete. In his playful innocence, he is reminiscent of Puck from *A Midsummer Night's Dream* or the storybook character Peter Pan. He is the embodiment of the Child in Transactional Analysis jargon.

SUGGESTED ADVICE: When the Fool appears in a client's spread, a fresh and innocent approach to some aspect of his life is trying to emerge. Encourage the client to open his mind to a more playful attitude both at work and recreation. Often, the mere fact that the Fool appears in the spread signals the readiness of the client for new adventure and curiosity in his life. Explore with the client the areas of his life which he feels are stagnant. Encourage an interjection of fun in those areas.

REVERSED MEANING: Here, the Fool is foolish, for his naivete has become exaggerated into disregard for reality. He is likely to act most unwisely in his excessive optimism about his plans. It would be best to wait and consider any action very logically and deliberately before taking risks.

I Le Bateleur · I Il Mago
I The Magician
I Der Magier · I El Mago

I THE MAGICIAN (Creative Intelligence)

UPRIGHT MEANING: The Magician has four tools available to manifest his will: the Sword of intellect, the Rod of inspiration, the Cup of emotion, and the Pentacle of practicality. These tools represent possible access to a variety of creative resources. They will lie wasted, however, unless the Magician focuses on manifesting his goal. He has the power to be original, independent, and strong-willed. When his creative powers are properly used, the Magician exemplifies the metaphysical truth that man creates his reality through his thoughts. Mind control and creative visualization represent the higher side of this ability. The serious student of metaphysics can use unseen forces to manifest positive thought on earth. In medieval times, alchemists worked with the energy of the Magician. Today, magicians who use illusion and sleight-of-hand demonstrate the skillful manipulation of the Magician card on a more mundane level. The inventor is another type of modern Magician.

SUGGESTED ADVICE: When the Magician appears in the client's spread, encourage him to draw upon his inventive abilities and to approach situations with creative and original solutions. If favorable cards appear with the Magician, the client is ready to trust his own resourcefulness and focused will. If he reaches a stumbling block, seemingly "magical" solutions can come to him intuitively. With a Court Card representing someone other than the client, the Magician can represent an independent person who has a streak of genius and who may inspire the client.

REVERSED MEANING: This card can refer to a person who is a "law unto himself," with little respect for the rights of others. He may behave erratically, refusing to honor his commitments. This selfish, headstrong behavior usually backfires on him, denying him the support of others. This person wants everything HIS way. He insists on his own freedom of expression at the expense of others. Often, he feels that his unique "genius" should allow him special rights in society.

II THE HIGH PRIESTESS
(Hidden Power)

UPRIGHT MEANING: The High Priestess represents depth and mystery. On the surface, she seems secretive and inscrutable. This is because she speaks only after going deep within herself for greater insight. She is able to tap into psychic, intuitive levels, easily reading people's motives. Sometimes she knows people better than they know themselves. She may appear so reserved that others think her unapproachable. Those who desire depth and insight, however, find her eager to share her gifts. Often, she gravitates towards a profession as a counselor or psychic reader in order to help people through her wisdom. She has often been associated with the Egyptian goddess Isis and the Virgin Mary. Like them, she acts as a mediator between God's feminine side and mankind. The Fairy Godmother and Good Fairy are representative of her power to grant wishes and effect miracles.

SUGGESTED ADVICE: This card shows an intriguing and mysterious woman in the client's life. Often past middle age, she has sex appeal and charisma but may be very discriminating about intimate involvements. She may come across as a *femme fatale*, desired by all but possessed by none. Her Mona Lisa inscrutability may be maddening yet fascinating to the client. He would do well to approach her with openness and sincerity if he hopes to gain her trust. In a woman's spread, this card challenges her to draw on her own inner depth and intuitive awareness.

REVERSED MEANING: The reversed High Priestess can show shallowness and superficiality, calling for a need to look deeper into situations for insight. It can also refer to manipulation and calculated intrigue for selfish reasons. Often, this card represent a woman who misuses her intuitive abilities by secretly manipulating and controlling others.

III L'Impératrice   III L'Imperatrice
III The Empress
III Die Herrscherin   III La Emperatriz

III THE EMPRESS (Fertility)

UPRIGHT MEANING: The Empress symbolizes Mother Nature in all her fruitfulness and abundance. She fosters growth in the physical and material world through the conception and birth of children, physical nurturing, and material prosperity. She represents comfort, luxury, and an easy enjoyment of life. The abundance which the Empress symbolizes is like a cornucopia of all of earth's bounty. When this card appears in a spread, it often represents the client's mother or a nurturing person around the client, such as a wife. She is usually a traditional type of woman who values home and family. She appreciates owning fine things and often takes an interest in cultural and social affairs. She can be a gracious hostess, an efficient homemaker, and a loving wife and mother. She is the flower of femininity, the symbol of growth, abundance, and prosperity.

SUGGESTED ADVICE: When the client is a woman, this card can symbolize her own femininity and fertility. With the **Three of Cups,** it can represent pregnancy. Suggest that the client look at how she can express her creativity or nurturing qualities more effectively. If the client is a man, the Empress symbolizes a woman around him who will nurture and care for him. The cards surrounding the Empress will indicate in what area the growth will take place; if Pentacles, money; if Cups, love and friendship; if Rods, creativity; if Swords, mental perception; if a Major Arcana card, consciousness. The archetypal femininity of the Venus de Milo, the graciousness of the southern belle, and the domesticity of Betty Crocker all capture the essence of the Empress.

REVERSED MEANING: Here, the Empress's natural love of pleasure and ease degenerates into laziness, hedonism, promiscuity, and financial extravagance. She goes to excess in self-indulgence and becomes vain and superficial. She is likely to spoil her loved ones with too much of what they want instead of wisely giving what is needed.

IV THE EMPEROR (Order)

UPRIGHT MEANING: The Emperor represents the male principle of logic, system, order, and a left-brained approach to life. He symbolizes authority figures of all kinds: fathers, bosses, executives, leaders, politicians, and statesmen. He is law and order as each of us confronts it in our everyday lives, whether in the form of a traffic ticket or a reprimand from our boss. He often relates to the way in which the client perceived his own father, as a fair

arbitrator of law and order or as the dictatorial tyrant. You might associate him with Alexander the Great, Winston Churchill, Julius Caesar, William the Conqueror, Napoleon, George Washington, or Queen Elizabeth I.

SUGGESTED ADVICE: When this card appears in a spread, an issue of jurisdiction or authority will arise in which the client must confront his attitudes toward outside power. If he has been rebellious in the past, he may overreact to the need for rules. If he has been over-intimidated by authority in the past, he may experience anxiety about pleasing authority figures in the upcoming situation.

REVERSED MEANING: This represents a person who has abused his power and authority, or a situation involving such abuse. The person has become tyrannical, domineering, or arbitrary in his decisions. Often he is an egomaniac concerned only with proving his power, while others suffer and offer lip service to him.

V Le Pape   V II Papa
V The Hierophant
V Der Hohepriester   V El Papa

V THE HIEROPHANT (Spiritual Rules)

UPRIGHT MEANING: The Hierophant represents the priests and dogma of organized religion. The need for an outside authority to interpret God's law for the masses was a powerful force in medieval Europe, where the earliest known Tarot decks originated. The need to be told by an external authority what was morally right and wrong was taken for granted in those times. Now, in the Age of Aquarius, with the rise of individualism and independent moral responsibility, we are moving away from rigid adherence to outside rules, in favor of individual moral standards and a personal experience of God. Private meditation and self-awareness techniques appeal now to more and more people because of the authenticity of decisions based on one's own conscience. The Hierophant shows a reliance on organized religion for spiritual support or for social acceptance. It often indicates a conventional and traditional mindset, one not very open to innovative ideas outside rigid perimeters. It can represent stubborn adherence to worn out beliefs and a fear of stepping outside of those safe beliefs to question and grow.

SUGGESTED ADVICE: Advise the client that he may be in a rut in his thinking, and need input from a new and previously rejected source. He might try reading a book on a new subject, or really listening to someone whose ideas and opinions differ radically from his own. He must realize that considering new ideas does not necessarily mean that he has to accept them. Old values die slowly and exposing himself to new ideas will allow him to gradually accept a new tolerance and breadth of vision.

REVERSED MEANING: The client has become stale and bored with his "safe" set of values and beliefs. He is ready to break out of old habits and ruts in his thinking. It is time for him to seek out groups and ideas that intrigued him in the past but that inertia and fear of change kept him from pursuing. Perhaps he should try a New Age religion, such as Unity, Unitarian, or First Church of Religious Science.

VI THE LOVERS (The Attraction of Choice)

UPRIGHT MEANING: The Lovers represents the urge to experience duality through relationship with the opposite sex. In Jungian psychology, this would symbolize the projection of the animus or anima upon the person of the opposite sex in order to integrate those opposite qualities in oneself. It is the experience of falling in love with oneself in the other person. This often provokes an awesome conflict as we both accept and reject those qualities in the beloved that are opposite to our own. The Lovers card can symbolize intense, passionate karmic attractions — the type of magnetic attraction that knows no logic or reason for being. Romeo and Juliet and the Duke and Duchess of Windsor are typical of the Lovers card in the fatal and compelling nature of their relationships. The Lovers card can also relate to making a difficult but correct choice between two very appealing alternatives.

SUGGESTED ADVICE: When the Lovers card appears in a client's spread, the client will be presented with a very appealing situation which he must accept or reject. Very likely, it will be a relationship that attracts him magnetically and that involves past life karma. Advise the client to be as aware as possible of the qualities within himself that he is projecting on his lover. Caution him about being seduced by the magnetism and passion in the relationship without seeing the elements of true compatibility for what they are. If he sees clearly, he will choose wisely. If not, he will merely see his new reflection in the mirror of another's face.

REVERSED MEANING: This card represents an unhealthy relationship based on a jealous, possessive, devouring love. This type of love can be both obsessive and destructive. It aims to control the other person rather than giving him the space to be himself. Often one or both of the partners are immature and have selected each other solely out of sexual attraction rather than love.

VII Le Chariot   VII Il Carro
VII The Chariot
VII Der Triumphwagen   VII El Carro

VII THE CHARIOT (Motivation)

UPRIGHT MEANING: The picture of the warrior charging forward in the chariot pulled by two sphinxes depicts the high energy and drive of this card. The Chariot represents focused energy and concentration on a goal. It is a card of action, assertiveness, and purpose. The harnessing of the energy of the passions to serve the goals of the ego produces the formidable energy and momentum of the Chariot. Spiritually, this card shows the physical, emotional, and mental bodies harnessed as servants of the will. Highly motivated sales people often display this go-getter, self-starter type of energy. Indiana Jones of *Raiders of the Lost Ark* also conveys the self-sufficiency and drive of the Chariot type of person. Sometimes, the Chariot relates to cars and vehicles of all kinds because of its relationship to movement and activity. Often, a trip, especially one by car, is indicated by the Chariot.

SUGGESTED ADVICE: When the Chariot appears in a spread, advise the client to proceed full speed ahead on any project that he feels strongly motivated to pursue. He has the energy and drive to accomplish his goal and must focus his concentration on it until he has succeeded.

REVERSED MEANING: Here, the Chariot is like a runaway car, representing reckless action and disregard for the rights of others in pursuit of one's goals. The Chariot reversed often symbolizes a person who misuses power and shows no respect for law and order in his quest for achievement. Usually, this type of person is unsuccessful even though he is ruthless because he scatters his energies rather than focusing them. This card can also indicate car trouble.

VIII STRENGTH (Self-Reliance)

UPRIGHT MEANING: Traditionally, this card is depicted as a woman who has tamed a lion to the extent that she can put her hand in his mouth safely. This symbolizes the qualities of gentleness, healing, and inner strength. The Strength card represents the ability to cope with conflict or crisis with calm and quiet confidence — to bring harmony out of conflict. Mahatma Gandhi with his philosophy of passive resistance embodied these qualities by achieving his goals peacefully. This card is often associated with good health and those who heal others. It often relates to a desire to care for animals or children. This is not a card of a weakling, but rather a person who does not overstate his strength by bullying others. Certain forms of martial arts show this blend of potential ferocity, accurate timing, and calm conviction. Melanie from *Gone With the Wind* is a good example of a person who is a quiet tower of strength.

SUGGESTED ADVICE: When the Strength card appears in a client's spread, he is experiencing a feeling of good health and inner confidence. Advise him that he will "attract more flies with honey than vinegar" in his dealings with others and that kindness and firmness will help him at this time.

REVERSED MEANING: The client may feel physically drained and weakened by stress. His energies need to be built up through rest and healthy food. He may feel vulnerable and act aggressively to hide his fears and insecurities. He feels worn out on some level and needs encouragement to feel more energetic and positive.

IX L'Ermite   IX L'Eremita
IX The Hermit
IX Der Einsiedler   IX El Ermitaño

IX THE HERMIT (Guidance)

UPRIGHT MEANING: The Hermit holds the lamp of wisdom to guide others to greater awareness. He often represents a period of contemplation and meditation needed to digest and assimilate external input. There is a tendency to turn inwards in a serious and reclusive way to draw strength from one's own inner awareness and insights. The Hermit may come from without as a teacher or mentor who encourages discipline and study. The Hermit often signifies undertaking serious study and research by enrolling in school. Although the student may seek knowledge through the external source of education, the symbolic meaning of the Hermit really refers to self-discovery through inner reflection.

SUGGESTED ADVICE: Ask the client if he has been spending a lot of time alone thinking or studying something of interest to him. Try to determine what areas seriously interest him and encourage him to learn more about them. It might be a good time to take classes or to look to a teacher for direction. Encourage the client to meditate or read inspirational literature to deepen his insights.

REVERSED MEANING: It is likely that the person has literally become a hermit, cutting himself off too much from human contact and companionship. He may feel paranoid around other people and afraid of close relationships. Try to find out why the person has withdrawn so completely and why he feels he has to isolate himself like an island. It is important for him to reintegrate himself back into society and feel accepted by others.

X WHEEL OF FORTUNE
(Changing Cycles)

X Wheel of Fortune
Das Glücksrad   La Rueda de la Fortuna

X La Roue de la Fortune   X La Ruota della Fortuna

UPRIGHT MEANING: The picture on the Wheel of Fortune card looks a great deal like a wheel used in gambling. This illustrates its connection with luck, fate, and destiny. It reminds us that, in life, everything changes in cycles and has its season of ascendancy and decline. As astrologers know, timing is often more important than luck. We can flow wisely in any cycle if we understand its rhythm. Often, we are given a clue to the hidden purpose behind events through "synchronicity" or meaningful coincidences. After a few of these seeming coincidences, we begin to feel that the universe is trying to tell us something. If we pay attention and act on our intuitive understanding of these energies, we flow with the hidden meaning of the moment rather than limiting our vision to cause and effect. This allows unexpected lucky events to occur and often moves our lives into a new direction. The continual interaction of the yin and the yang, called the Tao in Eastern philosophy, relates to the up and down movement of the Wheel of Fortune.

SUGGESTED ADVICE: Ask the client if he has been experiencing a feeling of excited anticipation, as if something very lucky were about to happen. Explain that a new cycle is about to propel him forward in a surprising new direction. This may coincide with a lucky break or with a feeling that his luck has changed. In reality, his ability to adapt flexibly to change will determine whether he accepts the good luck that the universe offers him or sees it as a disruptive temptation.

REVERSED: This card can mean that a person is out of step with his own cycle and that his timing is out of sync. This can manifest as all kinds of petty annoyances, unexpected expenses, and minor setbacks. The person may feel that he has been beset with bad luck. In reality, he is being made aware that he is not in tune with the "here and now" and must center himself in his own rhythm and flow. He may gain greater insight by looking at how astrology, numerology, or biorhythms are affecting him.

XI JUSTICE (Balance)

UPRIGHT MEANING: This card portrays Justice as a woman holding a set of scales in one hand and a sword in the other. These objects signify her authority to enforce with the sword the fairness that she measures with her scales. This card can indicate legal or karmic justice. Sometimes karmic justice is difficult to recognize, particularly if a karmic situation began in a past life. This card can show that a seemingly unfair karmic situation is actually in balance, even though it may not be apparent in this lifetime. The Justice card signifies balanced judgment and appropriate resolution of inequity. If legal battles are involved, this card can indicate a judgment in the client's favor. The card of Justice also refers to proper balance, not necessarily in proportions of 50 to 50. At times, we are required to give more than our fair share of energy. At other times, we receive more than 50 percent from others. We must see beyond the letter of the law, realizing that the scales will balance in the end. When we lose our sense of proportion, even in a good quality, the lack of balance is unappealing. The desire to be accepted is out of balance in the ''goody two shoes,'' the social climber, and the people-pleaser. Proper money management is lopsided in both the miser and the spendthrift. The brilliant intellectual goes overboard when he loses touch with his feelings.

SUGGESTED ADVICE: When this card appears in a spread, explain that balance and fairness must appear in the client's experiences. If legal or karmic situations seem to be the issue, stress the need to temper justice with mercy. What the client feels he deserves often represents a self-centered, one-sided view of the matter. Suggest that the client ''walk in the other person's moccasins'' before passing final judgment on him.

REVERSED MEANING: This card can represent injustice in the form of bias, prejudice, or illegal activity. In karmic situations, past life associations may have led one person to take advantage of another. This person is now out of balance in some area of his life and wasting energy through excess. Often, the excess overcompensates for some lack in another area of life.

XII THE HANGED MAN
(Suspension)

XII Le Pendu   XII L'Appiccato
XII The Hanged Man
XII Der Erhängte   XII El Colgado

UPRIGHT MEANING: The traditional picture on this card portrays a man with a halo around his head, hanging crucified upside down on a wooden cross. The Hanged Man represents that stage in the Fool's journey when he must question the deeper meaning and purpose of his life. It represents a period of polarization, suspended animation and self-sacrifice. During this time, a person may feel out of step with his old beliefs and attitudes, but confused about the direction of his new life. It is as though he stands at life's crossroads. One road leads to the safe and comfortable past that has now lost its meaning. The other road leads towards faith in a new vision that will require him to take responsibility for his actions. He feels his life is suspended in time and space, as he gropes for answers that will turn his ambivalence into commitment. He must endure this lack of direction until he turns his personal will over to God through an act of faith and chooses the path of awareness. For many people, this card represents a major turning point in their lives. They always remember feeling forced to stay in a very restricted position long enough to see life from an entirely different perspective. This brings the enlightenment symbolized by the halo around the Hanged Man. The crucifixions of both Christ and St. Peter relate to the self-sacrifice each man must experience for himself in order to grow.

SUGGESTED ADVICE: When this card appears in a client's spread, he often feels that his life is on hold or has lost direction. He may be between jobs, relationships, or philosophies. Explain that this waiting period is necessary for him to see past his confusion and know his true priorities. He must have faith that the holding pattern in his life is only temporary and will lead him to his next step.

REVERSED MEANING: This card signals that the period of suspended animation, confusion, and testing is over. The client is ready for decisive action.

XIII La Mort   XIII La Morte
XIII Death
XIII Der Tod   XIII La Muerte

XIII DEATH (Transformation)

UPRIGHT MEANING: The traditional figure of the Grim Reaper charging on his black steed through a desolate wasteland conveys the necessity of clearing away any debris in our lives. The Death card signifies endings and new beginnings, in a natural way, just as winter must return the world to a dormant state before spring can bloom. The transformation implied in the Death card is not really a finality, but rather a change of form. Like the phoenix rising from the ashes, death is always followed by a resurrection and rebirth. In this sense, the Death card relates to reincarnation — death and rebirth. Within a single incarnation, there are periods of intense transformation which are psychological deaths. We die to a part of ourselves that is decaying and useless, grieving over the ending until the new beginning is in sight. The most positive way to handle the psychological experience of the Death card is to cooperate in re-evaluating and revamping the dying situation. Rarely does the card of Death signify an actual physical death.

SUGGESTED ADVICE: Usually, the appearance of the Death card in a spread will provoke some anxiety for the client. Reassure him that this card does not mean physical death, but the necessity for him to let go of certain decaying and dying situations in his life. Usually, he can identify the source of his grief. Explore his resistance to letting it pass out of his life so that new energy can be born. He must have faith that the death is paving the way for new, more appropriate forms. He must pass through an empty feeling to allow space for new life to emerge from the void.

REVERSED: When the Death card is reversed, it is likely that the situation that needs to be reversed has been going on for some time. The client is resisting needed transformation. He is holding onto decaying conditions and may be forced to change through circumstances. Encourage him to accept the process of release and experience fully his grief.

XIV TEMPERANCE (Moderation)

XIV La Tempérance XIV La Temperanza
XIV *Temperance*
XIV Die Mässigkeit   XIV Templanza

UPRIGHT MEANING: The traditional picture on this card is of an angel blending fire and water. She manages to avoid putting out the fire with the water or turning the water into steam. Fire symbolizes inspiration and intuition, while water symbolizes emotional feeling. The angel has discovered the alchemy of blending these elements in proper proportion. She is like the good cook who knows how much of each ingredient will blend together well. She has the innate, intuitive sense of timing and proportion that constitutes perfect temperance. We can emulate these qualities by understanding the hidden energies behind timing and moderation. By living and acting in the here and now, we take appropriate action rather than being enslaved by habit. We are awake in each moment and can develop a zen-like gift for diplomacy and timing. We inwardly know the right moment to speak or act. Our lives seem to flow effortlessly. Temperance means that we do not overdo or underdo. It implies that we exercise moderation in areas such as eating, drinking, smoking, dieting, or spending. The proper proportion of these things may change daily or momentarily. Temperance means that we are attuned to these changes.

SUGGESTED ADVICE: This card in a spread means that the client has learned certain lessons about patience and timing. He realizes the necessity for moderation in his life. With a Court card of the opposite sex, this card can mean that the client has attracted a compatible mate by being willing to live in the here and now without straining for results.

REVERSED MEANING: This is a card of over-reaction and impulsiveness. The client is out of sync with the flow of things. His sense of timing is off. He may be inclined to go on a binge in his actions or expect too much from a situation.

XV Le Diable   XV Il Diavolo
XV The Devil
XV Der Teufel   XV El Diablo

XV THE DEVIL (Temptation)

UPRIGHT MEANING: The traditional picture shows a man and woman bound by chains to a menacing looking creature with an inverted pentagram on his forehead. The chains are so loose that the couple could easily escape, but they seem unaware of this fact. Similarly, they could easily escape from the enslavement of their own weaknesses by choosing their higher natures over their baser instincts. The Devil card, for each person, represents his own particular character flaw. It is often what he is most attracted to doing. The Devil represents a distortion of a neutral quality. For example, enjoying sensual pleasure is healthy unless it degenerates into hedonism. Loving oneself is a joyful experience unless it becomes selfishness. Although Devil situations are hard to detect, we can recognize them by their seductiveness and the easy way we slip into them. We may know intuitively that we are making a mistake, but the attraction of the weakness is very strong. Dealing with this Achilles heel can be a major step in growth and understanding. If we stir ourselves out of laziness, comfort, and ease, often we move ahead with great momentum. The Shadow in Jungian psychology represents the weak, underdeveloped part of ourselves that we are challenged to overcome.

SUGGESTED ADVICE: When this card appears in a spread, ask the client how he is tempted to backslide or give in to a weakness. He may be trying to diet or deal with habits involving smoking, alcohol, or drugs. Sometimes, this card refers to a very attractive relationship that threatens to drag him down. Often, the client is absorbed in materialism to the extent that he has become greedy. Whatever the situation, caution him that the easy route can be dangerous because it will keep him trapped in his weakness. Suggest that he think deeply or meditate before acting compulsively.

REVERSED MEANING: With this card reversed, the client is fed up with his weakness and sees the trap involved in giving in to it. He is more inclined to overcome his stagnation in order to grow. He may need to prove to himself that he has outgrown his dependence on the weakness by overcoming temptation.

XVI THE TOWER (Catalyst for Change)

UPRIGHT MEANING: The lightning struck Tower is a graphic symbol for surprising events in life. The Tower indicates that our plans will not go as expected, which may ultimately be necessary for the benefit of all. If we have built our plans on shaky ground, this card can show a sudden breakdown in our plans. Our false sense of security crumbles and we are forced to rebuild out of chaos. The new structure will have a sturdier foundation based on experience and realism. Tower types of experiences often represent the hand of fate. They frequently correspond to natural disasters, accidents, bankruptcy, or physical, emotional, or mental collapse. Usually, we have had a hand in our own fate by pushing ourselves and our life situations to the point of sudden breakdown. Like Humpty Dumpty, the pieces will never fit together the same way but must be reassembled from the usable debris. Many lessons are learned about necessary limits after a calamity strikes. This restores a new sense of order. The volcanic destruction of Pompeii, the stock market crashes of 1929 and 1987, and Nixon's fall from power are examples of Tower experiences.

SUGGESTED ADVICE: When this card appears in a client's spread, he is unprepared for sudden reversals. He has been tempting fate by living on the edge of potential disaster in personal or financial affairs. He must restructure his affairs so that he is better prepared for the unexpected. Having trusted blindly that nothing would go wrong, the client is now tested by circumstances beyond his control. He must learn to combine prudence with optimism. If the client has planned wisely, the Tower in combination with very favorable cards can mean a windfall or surprising good luck.

REVERSED MEANING: Here, the handwriting is on the wall. The client is well aware that certain aspects of his life are crumbling. He must understand why his plans could not have succeeded and he must release a past mistake. He will most likely feel relieved that an impossible situation is over. His acceptance of this collapse will pave the way for new opportunities.

XVII L'Étoile   XVII La Stella
XVII The Star
XVII Der Stern   XVII La Estrella

XVII   THE STAR (Sense of Purpose)

UPRIGHT MEANING: The Star shown on this card is more than the star of hope. It is like the star of the Magi which leads us unerringly to our inner divinity. The woman on the card pours water from one hand into a pool of water. From the other hand, she pours water onto the earth. Symbolically, we must draw upon both the unconscious (represented by water) and conscious levels of ourselves (represented by the earth) to fully grow and express ourselves. The Star inspires us to reach for our highest potential: to reach for the stars. Sometimes, we attune to our highest potential through dreams, meditation, or visualization. Our wishes and dreams act as our own fairy godmother to help us actualize our life purpose. The Star relates to stars of all kinds on the physical plane — movie stars, astronomers, astrologers, UFO's, and extraterrestrials. When our lives have become stale and feel meaningless, we must attune to our higher selves for further nourishment and direction.

SUGGESTED ADVICE: When the Star appears in a spread, the client will be prompted to realign himself to his higher purpose. It may be a vision of his potential or career which he has had from childhood. Ask him what he can imagine for himself that would really inspire him. Encourage him to foster those dreams through work or hobbies. The Star also indicates that the client is in good health and is feeling optimistic.

REVERSED MEANING: This card shows disillusionment and hopelessness. The client has lost touch with his source of inspiration and is inclined to feel depressed and pessimistic. Try to discover the source of his purposelessness and offer hope to him. With the **Eight of Swords**, **Nine of Swords**, or **Ten of Swords**, this card can mean illness.

XVIII THE MOON (Hidden Forces)

XVIII La Lune   XVIII La Luna
XVIII The Moon
XVIII Der Mond   XVIII La Luna

UPRIGHT MEANING: The traditional picture on this card shows two dogs howling at the full moon. A lobster creeps from a dark pool of water onto the earth. This eerie landscape symbolizes those things that haunt us: our own secrets, buried memories, paranoias, and inner compulsions. These dark recesses of our minds emerge periodically into our awareness so that we can integrate them into our personalities. If we run away, they continue to pursue us, seeking acknowledgment. If we turn and face them, we discover they are our friends: facets of ourselves that we need to accept. Sometimes, this card relates to psychic experiences: hunches, out-of-body experiences, and mediumship. We may be tapping into our past lives through dreams of regression. Often, the Moon indicates that our emotions are activated through mood swings or mental instability. Through whatever means, the Moon card shows that the psychic, mysterious levels of the unconscious mind are emerging to be reconciled with the conscious mind.

SUGGESTED ADVICE: When this card appears in the spread, the client is dealing with unconscious forces within himself. He may be confused by subtle messages in the environment, or struggling to make sense of an unclear situation. He may be engaged in behind the scenes activity and have to keep a low profile. Advise him to release his frustration over his confusion and lack of clarity. Situations will gradually come into focus if he does not fearfully resist the process.

REVERSED MEANING: When this card is reversed, it represents a more serious threat, such as subversive activity, sabotage, or deliberate deception. Misunderstandings and the secret schemes of others to undermine the client will come to light. On the psychic level, the client may be the victim of psychic attack by an enemy or feel bad vibrations around him. With the **Seven of Swords**, the Moon can refer to theft, "rip off," or illegal acts. With the **Seven of Cups**, it can mean a dangerous involvement with drugs or alcohol.

XIX Le Soleil   XIX Il Sole
XIX The Sun
XIX Die Sonne   XIX El Sol

XIX THE SUN (Joy)

UPRIGHT MEANING: The traditional picture on this card shows the Sun bright in the sky, sunflowers blooming, and a happy child riding a white horse. This scene conveys satisfaction and the sheer joy of being alive. The Sun card is childlike in its optimism and exuberance for the simple pleasures of life. On an inner level, it refers to creative self-expression. We feel no inhibition or fear in radiating our unique potential. The Fool has successfully overcome his self-consciousness and returned to the spontaneous expression of his inner Sun or self. He is no longer foolish or naive, but has gained through experience the wisdom to express his true essence. He has learned to connect to his higher self and channel meaning and purpose through his personality. He becomes the source of light and life for others, radiating warmth to those around him. On an outer level, the Sun refers to honor, recognition, success, and fulfillment of goals.

SUGGESTED ADVICE: This card is always a happy card to find in a spread. It signifies contentment and achievement for the client. He is healthy, happy, and aware of the good things in his life. The surrounding cards will indicate the area where he feels most fulfilled. Encourage him to foster this positive frame of mind by spreading his joy and encouragement to others. His optimism and success could be infectious and serve as an inspiration to others.

REVERSED MEANING: This card operates in two ways. In the first way, success has gone to the client's head and he has become arrogant, flashy, and egotistical. He is immersed in the outer appearances of success and may not feel that he has to earn his recognition. In the second way, the client is pessimistic and negative in his thinking and has a strong sense of failure. With other health cards, this card can show illness or serious depression. Encourage the client to cultivate a more positive outlook on life.

XX JUDGMENT (Reward)

XX Le Jugement   XX Il Giudizio
XX Judgment
XX Das Gericht   XX El Juicio

UPRIGHT MEANING: The traditional picture on this card shows an angel sounding his trumpet in the sky as people on earth rise from the water to welcome him. It depicts a joyful resurrection in which the personality unites with the higher self or soul. In the area of spiritual development, it symbolizes the integration of one's higher consciousness into everyday awareness and the acceptance of the soul as the true inner person. The person awakens from the illusion that his happiness lies outside himself and becomes centered in the inner peace within. This card represents a balancing of karma because of valuable lessons learned. The person has sown his seeds wisely and can now reap his reward. With his reward comes the beginning of a new cycle of development and the chance to learn more lessons. Often, this card relates to a positive conclusion in a law suit or other legal matters, especially with **Justice,** the **Five of Rods R,** and Pentacle cards.

SUGGESTED ADVICE: This is a time for the client to awaken to some important realizations about his path in life. If he receives a tangible sign of his reward for work well done, advise him to look back at the steps that led up to his success. Encourage him to appreciate the wisdom of those actions that made the reward possible. Let him know that karmic situations are being rectified through these events and a new, more positive cycle is beginning.

REVERSED MEANING: Here, the client has not seen the lessons that he needs to learn. Consequently, he has exercised poor judgment in his actions. An external event, such as losing a law suit or incurring an unfavorable decision, may confirm this message from the universe. The event signals that he is incurring negative karma for failure to learn his lessons. This is not a punishment, but rather, an indication that he needs to see his errors and correct them.

XXI Le Monde   XXI Il Mondo
XXI The World
XXI Die Welt   XXI El Mundo

XXI THE WORLD (Synthesis)

UPRIGHT MEANING: In the traditional picture on this card, a woman holding two rods dances in a wreath. The wreath is surrounded by the symbols for the four fixed signs of the zodiac: Taurus the bull, Leo the lion, Scorpio the eagle, and Aquarius the man. This card represents the ability to blend together the best qualities of these four signs. It represents the ability to overcome the stubbornness and preoccupation with material and physical comfort of Taurus; the self-centeredness, pride, and arrogance of Leo; the obsessiveness with sex, money, and power of Scorpio; and the lack of both commitment and cooperation of Aquarius. This card shows the ability to dance to a distant drummer by listening intuitively to the pulse of the universe. It shows the ability to rise above attachment to the material plane through attunement to the inner voice. The dancer on this card balances the physical and spiritual planes perfectly in her dance, as symbolized by the rods she holds. The Fool's journey is complete with this card. He has found meaning and purpose in the myriad different experiences he has encountered. This card often relates to travel, especially international or long distance travel, if combined with the **Six of Swords**, the **Knight of Rods**, the **Eight of Rods**, the **Fool**, or the **Wheel of Fortune**.

SUGGESTED ADVICE: The client is approaching a situation in which he can handle all elements very well. He may become aware of a new mastery over the situation. Encourage him to pull together all the different facets involved and to blend them together harmoniously. The cards nearby will show the type of situation: mental (Swords), emotional (Cups), financial (Pentacles), or creative (Rods).

REVERSED MEANING: The client is on the brink of tying together loose ends to see the total picture. However, he still has limited understanding of the situation. He is eager to experience a broader picture but must take the necessary steps to finish the cycle. At this point, he must complete unfinished business and follow through with his goals.

THE BLANK CARD (The Unknowable)

MEANING: The blank or extra card represents the secrets we want or need to keep from ourselves during a reading. The Hanson-Roberts deck has a dedication card, called "To All Believers," that can be used for this purpose. Even with a tool as invaluable as the Tarot, there are finite limits to the information we can access through it. Often, it would not be in our best interests to know too much about the future of a certain situation. We must encounter it without preconceived notions. Sometimes, our higher selves and unconscious minds are aware that we would miss out on the joy of exploration and discovery if we failed to unravel the mystery for ourselves. When the blank card appears in a spread, we may read the meanings of other cards in the spread, but we must trust our own instincts and intuitive promptings to carry us deeper into our quest. We must realize that we may be led into uncharted territory where the possibilities are endless. A question that elicits the blank card often involves new growth. We may feel we are leaping into the void but, with this card present, the experience may prove very enriching. After a week or so, or whenever the surrounding conditions have changed, the client may want to ask the Tarot again for information on this issue. If the blank card no longer appears, he is allowed to look more clearly at the unfolding picture. Basically, by adding this extra card to the Tarot deck, we give the cards a means of letting us know our limitations in our readings. When this card appears repeatedly in spreads for a client, it signals to the reader that it is best for the client to receive only limited input at this time in terms of prediction. The reader may counsel the client based on the other cards that fall, but would be most helpful by withholding strong indications about the future. In these instances, usually the client needs to talk about his problems so that he can gradually sort them out.

Combinations

Three or Four of a Kind in a Spread

Since there are four Aces through Kings in the deck, at times you will see three or four of the same numbered or Court card in a spread. When this happens, it reinforces the basic meaning of the type of card involved. For example, with three or four Aces, the emphasis is on new beginnings. The meanings are summarized here.

Three or Four ACES	New beginnings
Three or Four TWOS	Duality, choices, decisions, and partnership
Three or Four THREES	Creativity, synthesis, self-expression, and collaboration
Three or Four FOURS	Solid foundation and security
Three or Four FIVES	Change, variety, and insecurity
Three or Four SIXES	Responsibility, home, work, and stability
Three or Four SEVENS	Reevaluation, deeper insight, and change of perspective
Three or Four EIGHTS	Power, control, organization, and mastery of a situation
Three or Four NINES	Fulfillment or completion of a cycle
Three or Four TENS	The ultimate abundance or excess
Three or Four PAGES	News, communication, thoughts, and children

Three or Four KNIGHTS	Coming and going, travel, and quick action
Three or Four QUEENS	Women or female influence in society
Three or Four KINGS	Men or male influence in society

Preponderance of Suits

You may also see spreads where half or more of the cards are in one suit. On these occasions, you should emphasize the suit's basic meaning in your reading.

If **Cups** are the dominant suit, the spread highlights emotional matters, love, and affection.

If over half the cards are **Pentacles**, the spread emphasizes financial and business matters.

If the majority of the cards are **Swords**, the spread is chiefly about courage, will, and potential stress or conflict.

With a majority of **Rods**, the emphasis is on creativity, inspiration, and enterprise.

Preponderance of Major Arcana Cards

If half or more cards in a spread are Major Arcana cards, there are levels to the question that are subtle and lie beneath the surface. Psychological and spiritual meanings are often more important than the superficial events or happenings surrounding the question. In these instances, go over the meaning of each Major Arcana card in the spread carefully. Then ask yourself, "Why is this issue so problematic or challenging for me to deal with? What are my hopes, fears, and expectations?" Often, it takes much soul searching to understand the deeper meaning that the cards are trying to reveal to you.

Other Combinations

People often wonder how a reader sees major life changes such as death or divorce in a spread. No single card signifies an event of this magnitude. It takes several cards combined in a spread to trigger the possible interpretation of events such as birth, marriage, death, or accident.

The following list shows certain combinations that indicate specific meanings. You should see at least two or three of the cards shown in the combination before interpreting them as listed. For example, the combination for surgery or heart trouble is Three of Swords, Eight of Swords, Nine of Swords, Tower, or Star R. You would not interpret this as surgery or heart trouble unless two, but more likely three or more of the above cards were together in the spread.

Be cautious about interpreting negative cards for another person in an alarming or frightening way. If you saw the combination for surgery or heart trouble in a spread, it would be best to ask the person if he has any health problems and warn him to pay special attention to health in the near future.

ALCOHOLISM OR DRUGS	Three of Cups R Seven of Cups Temperance R Moon R
ARGUMENTS	Three of Swords Five of Swords Five of Rods Seven of Rods Ten of Cups R
BIRTH OR PREGNANCY	Three of Cups Six of Cups Page of Cups Empress
CAR ACCIDENT	Eight of Swords Nine of Swords Ten of Swords Chariot R Wheel of Fortune R Tower
CAR, PURCHASE OF	Ace of Pentacles Chariot Empress

COMPUTERS, HIGH TECH	Chariot Magician Hierophant R
DATE, SOCIAL INVITATION	Three of Cups Page of Cups Knight of Cups
DIET, SUCCESS OF	Seven of Cups R Strength Devil R Temperance Justice
DIVORCE	Three of Swords Four of Rods R Ten of Pentacles R Tower Death Judgment Justice
ENLIGHTENMENT	Ace of Pentacles or Cups Star Tower Magician High Priestess
GAY PERSON	Page of Cups Queens (for males) Kings or Knights (for females)
HEALTH, GOOD	Strength Star Sun
HEALTH, HOSPITALIZATION	Four of Swords Eight of Swords Star R

HEALTH, RETURN TO	Four of Swords R Star No high Swords (Eight, Nine, or Ten)
HEALTH, SEVERE PROBLEM OR POSSIBLE DEATH	Four of Swords Ten of Swords Death Tower Star R
HEALTH, SURGERY OR HEART TROUBLE	Three of Swords Eight of Swords Nine of Swords Tower or Star R
HOME, CHANGE OF	Four of Rods R Nine of Pentacles R Knight of Rods Tower
JOB, LOSS OF OR LAYOFF	Five of Pentacles Seven of Pentacles R Tower
JOB, QUITTING	Pentacles Three of Swords High Swords (Eight, Nine, or Ten) Eight of Cups
JOB, RAISE OR PROMOTION	Six of Pentacles Seven of Pentacles Sun
KARMA, BAD	Devil Wheel of Fortune R Magician R Judgment R
KARMA, GOOD	Six of Cups Six of Pentacles

LAWSUIT	Five of Rods
	Judgment
	Justice
MARRIAGE	Three of Cups
	Four of Rods
	Ten of Pentacles
	Ten of Cups
	Lovers
MEDITATION	Hermit
	High Priestess
	Star
MONEY, LOSS OF OR BAD INVESTMENT	Seven of Swords
	Seven of Pentacles R
	Nine of Pentacles R
	Ten of Pentacles R
	Sun R
	Empress R
MONEY, RICHES	Nine of Pentacles
	Ten of Pentacles
	Sun
	Empress
MONEY, WINNING A PRIZE	Pentacles
	Six of Pentacles
	Sun
	Wheel of Fortune
NEWS, GOOD	Eight of Rods
	Page of Rods
RIP-OFF	Five of Swords
	Seven of Swords
	Seven of Cups
	Devil
	Moon R
STUDENT OR SCHOOL	Three of Pentacles
	Eight of Pentacles
	Hermit

THEFT

Pentacles
Five of Swords
Seven of Swords
Nine of Pentacles R

TRAVEL

Six of Swords
Eight of Rods
Knight of Rods
World
Fool
Wheel of Fortune

WISHES FULFILLED

Six of Rods
Nine of Cups
Star
Sun

Celtic Cross Spread

A spread is any specific arrangement of cards in which the positions of the cards indicate certain meanings such as past, present, future, or final outcome.

The basic spread most often used is called the *Celtic Cross Spread* because the cards form a cross in the center with a row of cards to the right. The diagram for this spread shows both the meanings of the positions and the order in which you deal cards, beginning with 1 and ending with 10.

Meanings of Positions in the Spread

As the diagram shows, the **1st** and **2nd** cards represent the present situation involved in the question.

The **3rd** card describes the foundation or basis of the matter. It can indicate whether your question is based on a stable or shaky set of feelings and circumstances.

The **4th** card represents how the past relates to the question. This could be recent past or distant past, especially if the person is still working through related issues from long ago.

The **5th** card tells you how the situation appears on the surface to you or the general public. Based on other cards in this spread, this appearance may or may not be accurate.

The **6th** card is the next event or change in the situation.

The **7th** card reveals your hidden psychological reactions to the question, or the unrevealed destiny involved in the issue.

The **8th** card reveals how relationships with other people involved in the situation will affect the question.

The **9th** card tells your conscious thoughts or expectations about the matter. It helps you become aware of how positive or negative you are about the matter involved.

The **10th** card is the final outcome. It indicates the likely resolution of the situation based on the past and present as it exists now. If you radically change your approach to the issue involved, you will alter the final outcome and a new spread will be required.

An Example

This examples takes one Major Arcana card, the Tower, through each position of the Celtic Cross Spread to see how its meaning shifts slightly in each position.

In position **1** or **2**, the Tower indicates that the structure of the situation is presently shaky and subject to unexpected change. This might well be for the best if the question was based on a false sense of security.

In position **3**, the entire foundation or basis of the question is insecure. It is likely either to fall apart or to undergo unexpected change.

In position **4**, the past of the situation was unstable and insecure. It may have already changed unexpectedly or appeared to fall apart.

In position **5**, the situation seems to be ready to fall apart. This may or may not be true based on the rest of the cards in the Spread. Remember position 5 is only the outward appearance or superficial image of the situation.

In position **6**, the next important event will be an unexpected upheaval or crumbling of plans.

In position **7**, the destiny of the situation may be fated to undergo change or fall apart. There may be hidden circumstances involved in the issue.

In position **8**, a relationship involved in the situation will shake it up considerably and threaten to destroy it or to change it into a radically different form.

In position **9**, your conscious mind expects a jolt or surprising turn of events. You are aware that your plans may fall apart or changes may happen.

In position **10**, the events and factors revealed in the other positions in the spread lead to a drastic change of plans, which will be brought on by false security or unexpected events. You will have to adjust to these changes and rebuild the situation in a different way.

Double Celtic Cross Spread

This spread is just like the basic Celtic Cross Spread except that it has a second layer of cards next to each position in the Celtic Cross Spread. In addition, there are separate cards for timing and for the advice of the cards. The diagram "Double Celtic Cross Spread" shows the order in which the cards are laid out in this spread. Notice that you place only one additional card rather than two in the center. Each of the other additional cards are placed alongside the original card. To interpret this kind of spread, blend the meanings of the two cards in each position.

The Timing and Advice Cards

The Tarot reader acts as the intermediary between the universal mind and the client. The Tarot does not and will not reveal all that the client would like to know — only the information he *should know* to handle most successfully the situation in question. Knowing that his situation is heading for a fortunate conclusion may well encourage the client to sit back and wait for his "good luck," instead of taking the intermediate steps to guarantee success. This is why the timing card and the advice of the cards are so helpful to the reader. Both are useful in answering two frequent questions of clients: "When will the situation change?" and "What should I do now about the situation?"

Timing

The timing card gives the time interval covered by the spread. The suit indicates whether the duration is a matter of days, weeks, or months:

Cups   — days

Rods   — weeks

Pentacles   — months

The number of the card indicates the number of days, weeks, or months involved:

Ace through Ten — one through ten

Page   — eleven

Knight   — twelve

To determine the timing, combine the suit and numerical value of the card. For example, the Page of Cups in the timing position is 11 days, the 10 of Pentacles is 10 months.

In some cases, timing cannot be determined or is based on a client's decision to take action. This is true if any of the following appears in the timing position:

Swords   — undetermined, up to you

Queen   — undetermined, up to you

King   — undetermined, up to you

If a Major Arcana card falls in the timing position, it indicates that the client is involved in an ongoing psychological process. The process has already begun and is proceeding in the present.

Major Arcana   — now

If the timing card is very immediate, such as the next two weeks, the reader must emphasize the best advice of the cards, because the cards do not want to reveal the outcome beyond that time. Often, this is because the client must grapple with an important test or lesson in his personal growth during the time period. The Major Arcana cards in the spread will often describe the lesson involved.

It is not necessary to interpret the meaning of the timing card, but often the card that falls there is very appropriate to the situation.

The Advice of the Cards

The ''advice of the cards'' position tells you the best approach or attitude for handling the question. Since the Double Celtic Cross Spread gives so much information, often the reader really needs one card that simplifies and summarizes the best approach for the client to take right now about the issue. The ''advice of the cards'' slot fulfills this need.

Celtic Cross Spread

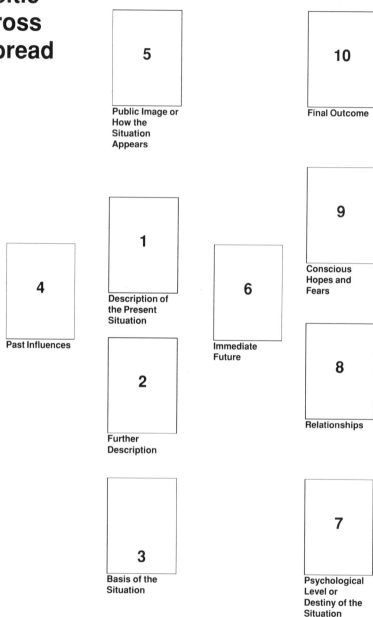

5
Public Image or How the Situation Appears

10
Final Outcome

1
Description of the Present Situation

9
Conscious Hopes and Fears

4
Past Influences

6
Immediate Future

2
Further Description

8
Relationships

3
Basis of the Situation

7
Psychological Level or Destiny of the Situation

Double Celtic Cross Spread

14	5

Public Image or
How the
Situation
Appears

19	10

Final Outcome

	1

Description of
the Present
Situation

13	4

Past Influences

15	6

Immediate
Future

18	9

Conscious
Hopes and
Fears

11	2

Further
Description

17	8

Relationships

20

Timing

12	3

Basis of the
Situation

21

Advice of the
Cards

16	7

Psychological
Level or
Destiny of the
Situation

The Ethics of Reading for Others

Helping Others with the Tarot

The old saying "Knowledge is power" is doubly true in using the Tarot. The question of using that power ethically needs examination when you are reading the cards for other people. As a reader, you hold a great deal of power to influence other people, because of the mystique and magic of gaining hidden knowledge through 78 pasteboard cards. People tend to hang on every word you utter in a card reading. This necessitates a very careful choice of words and the highest of motives.

Motives and Intentions

It is important to be clear in your own mind about your motives and intentions before reading a deck of Tarot cards for others. Some useful objectives might be:

- helping the client gain greater depth, insight, and objectivity into his situation

- helping him understand his responsibility and his relationship to the situation

- helping him discover new solutions to old problems

- seeing other people's motives objectively

- educating people about the value of the Tarot as a tool for inner growth and awareness.

The Role of Psychology and Counseling

The Tarot can be considered more of a counseling tool than a fortunetelling device. The insight and skills necessary to properly translate and interpret the Tarot symbols are very similar to counseling techniques. A knowledge of both psychology and counseling is really needed to handle intelligently the responsibility of reading cards for others. This knowledge will allow you to phrase your interpretation of the cards so that the average client can relate to them and grow from them.

When reading cards for a client, it helps to emphasize the psychological aspects of the information rather than events. This puts in the hands of the client the power to change his life through awareness and growth. Putting yourself in the position of the High Priest or Priestess with all the answers could promote dependency in clients and set you up as responsible for the success or failure of their actions. It helps to remind yourself that, as a reader, you are an interpreter or translator of the client's unconscious mind. Your role is to feed this hidden knowledge of himself back to him for consideration.

Emphasize the person-centered or subjective meanings of the cards in addition to the event-oriented or objective meanings. To a large extent, our perception of our reality *is* our reality. Don't ignore the events that appear in a Tarot reading, but prepare the client for his reactions and feelings about an event. This will provide a psychological cushion before its actual occurrence.

For example, you may see in the cards that the client will receive a large sum of money in the near future. You may also see that this windfall will bring out the client's tendency toward extravagance and gambling. By warning him about his likely reaction to this event, you may help the client overcome his weakness and further his growth. You will have done more than predict an event which would happen anyway regardless of the client's foreknowledge. You will have given the client insight into his own character and weaknesses.

Making Predictions

The question of making predictions is another ethical issue with Tarot reading. Try to make it very clear to the client that his thoughts and attitudes greatly influence the course of events in his life. The answer to his questions in a spread indicates the way events will *tend* to go in the future if he keeps on doing what he is presently doing. Emphasize to the client that he is in the driver's seat in his life. Try to encourage him to exercise his personal power in his life situations.

Many clients will try to pass this responsibility back to you. When that occurs, it is best to state that you are not a fortuneteller, but a counselor who uses the Tarot as a tool to help people. Because Tarot reading is so often associated with fortunetelling by the general public, it is wise to tell clients before the appointment, verbally or through a typed sheet, your philosophy and approach to reading the future with the cards. This direct approach to the issue of predicting will eliminate clients who are seeking only what is going to happen to them instead of being open to how they can influence their own lives.

Delivering Bad News Tactfully and Helpfully

Like every Tarot reader, you will encounter situations in readings in which you see from the cards that your client is headed for a crisis. Unlike an ordinary counselor who does not see the future, you hold a double-edged sword when you see difficulties ahead and are faced with the responsibility of preparing your client for them.

The important thing is to give the client the information he needs as reflected by the cards, rather than the information he wants. What most people want to know from a reader is a direct function of how well or poorly they handle the challenges presented to them on the way to their goals.

While no client wants to hear bad news, if you omit or whitewash potential trouble ahead, you are shirking your responsibility to your client and may incur his resentment when the problem arises in reality. At the same time, you must deliver the news in a tactful way that helps the client see choices and possible alternatives. Diplomacy and tact are very necessary when reading negative cards in spreads for others.

Avoiding Dire Predictions

People often ask whether a reader should predict "bad" things like death, accident, or divorce. You should avoid at all costs a "doom and gloom" approach to card reading. Because of the power of thought to influence life, never unequivocally predict a "bad" event. If the cards do look critical, prepare the client for a worsening or deterioration of the situation, but always with encouragement as to how he can best handle or improve it. Don't let the client leave thinking that a certain event is preordained and therefore out of his control.

Refusing to Invade the Privacy of Others

Some clients may ask you to snoop or spy on other people. For example, they may want to know if their lover is faithful or if someone will die and leave them money. There is a very gray area of ethics in the situation of violating another person's privacy with the Tarot. The key to this sticky issue is the motive of the person asking the question. Is the motive to manipulate someone else out of self-interest, or is it goodwill and concern, such as a mother asking about the welfare of her children?

Other people appear regularly in the cards of clients, since no one lives in a vacuum. Clients are entitled to this information in their reading. It is only when they ask a question about someone else that the reader must decide whether allowing that question is a misuse of the Tarot. Keeping the reading focused on the client and his own personal sphere of influence tends to discourage snooping and invasion of privacy.

As a general rule of thumb, to avoid compromising your own sense of ethics and fairness or violating another person's rights, the Golden Rule is a good standard to use for judging ethical situations. Your intuition or your gut feeling will often warn you away from compromising situations in reading cards. Learn to trust yourself and don't be afraid to say "No" to a client's request for confidential information. You as the reader are the keeper of the keys to the kingdom which the Tarot unveils.

Accepting Money for Readings

The issue of accepting money for reading Tarot cards is difficult for many people. Charging for readings encourages you as a reader to take your responsibility seriously, fine-tune your skills, and increase your competency. To keep a skill at the amateur level often fosters mediocrity. Slapdash methods are easily rationalized away by not accepting money for the service. Often professional readers hear from their clients of being traumatized by the "doom and gloom" readings they have received from a friend who is an amateur card reader. A person whose business involves rendering a service is selling time as well as skill and expertise. This service deserves some form of payment.

The Unknowable

The Blank Card

Although the Tarot can give us access to vast stores of hidden information, many people believe that we are not meant to know certain things ahead of time. You can allow the cards to indicate these instances by putting an extra blank card in the deck to specifically mean "the unknowable, a secret we need to keep from ourselves." Most decks of Tarot cards come packaged with an extra blank card. You can also use any card that has the same design on the back as the rest of the deck.

This technique works very well because it acts as a red flag when a question has hit a forbidden area where certain information will be withheld. The restriction may be only temporary so that, in time, the Tarot will release the information in another spread.

What We Don't Yet Understand About the Tarot

Objective and Subjective Reality

Most people who read cards regularly notice that, at times, the cards "talk" clearly and explicitly to them. At other times, the cards seem to be confusing or blocked. Modern quantum physics has revealed that man constantly influences his environment and interacts with it in a reciprocal way. The scientist in the laboratory influences his experiment by his very presence and being. This implies that there is really not a sharp distinction between objective and subjective reality. If not, what are the cards really telling us?

Are the cards compensatory, reflecting back to us our own unconscious viewpoint, or are they objectively accurate and predictive? Can we control the kinds of answers we get from the Tarot by using the will, and thereby coerce it into telling us what we want to hear?

The Conscious and Unconscious

Certain people with very strong wills can overrule the unconscious in favor of their conscious wishes and bend answers from the Tarot to their wills. In these cases, they undermine the accuracy of their answer and receive only what they want to hear from the Tarot. It is similar to trying too hard to dream about a certain thing. The harder you try, the less relaxed you are to let a natural process take over. The best way to counteract this tendency is for the person to phrase his question before he begins shuffling and clear his mind while he shuffles. This allows the unconscious mind to operate. Tarot readings are usually compensatory to what we consciously think. In other words, they show us our hidden thoughts and feelings. The sections of a spread that deal with the past and present of a situation will usually reflect our conscious thinking on the matter. The rest of the spread reveals what our higher self knows about the present and future of the question.

Jung believed that we must pay attention to both conscious and unconscious feedback to be well-rounded in our awareness. Going overboard in either direction leads to distortion and misperception of our reality and experience. Depending on how centered we are when we shuffle the cards, we give our unconscious free rein to express itself or to repress the flow somewhat. When we feel centered and flowing rather than anxious and fearful of an undesired answer, our readings are more informative, insightful, and accurate. When we're uptight about something, the Tarot functions as a barometer of our own insecurities and fears.

We can accept the input from the unconscious via the Tarot reading much as we would interpret a dream. However, we must also pay attention to what our conscious mind is telling us about the issue. Too much reliance upon the feedback from the Tarot fosters excessive dependency upon the Tarot and the unconscious to handle every decision. It weakens the will and confidence in the ego's ability to cope, and turns the reins of life over to the unconscious.

Free Will and Predestination

The predictive side of the Tarot raises many unexplained questions, such as the issue of free will versus predestination. Why is it that the Tarot predicts events so literally and accurately at times, while at other times, events don't happen as expected?

One view is that there is a strong tendency and momentum for events to follow the line of least resistance. It takes an effort of will to go against the inertia of following that tendency to its conclusion. In astrology, we say, "Character is destiny," meaning that one can predict what a person will do in a situation if we know enough about his motivations, needs, and character. The same applies in reading Tarot cards. Most people will follow the path of habit instead of breaking the pattern. For this reason, we can assume that the future tendency of events will probably literally manifest itself. However, if a person breaks his usual pattern because of a fuller awareness, his thoughts and attitudes change and future events will reflect this change in himself.

There seem to be some events in everyone's life that are destined to occur, but they are few compared to those we can affect through free will. Perhaps, even those destined events are chosen by us before we incarnate each time.